RESEARCH REPORT   JUNE 2015

A First Look at the 5Essentials in Illinois Schools

Joshua Klugman, Molly F. Gordon, Penny Bender Sebring, Susan E. Sporte

TABLE OF CONTENTS

1 Executive Summary

3 Introduction

Chapter 1
5 Exploring the Five Essential Supports in Illinois Schools

Chapter 2
13 How the Essential Supports Vary across Communities, School Types

Chapter 3
19 How the Essential Supports Relate to Student Outcomes

Chapter 4
27 Interpretive Summary

31 References

34 Appendices A–B

ACKNOWLEDGEMENTS

The authors would like to thank the Illinois State Board of Education (ISBE), and in particular Peter Godard, for his insight and thoughtful comments on the potential policy implications of this work. In addition, we would like to acknowledge Julie Evans and Shuwan Chiu at ISBE for providing us the data that allowed us to do this work. We also thank the Steering Committee members of the University of Chicago Consortium on Chicago School Research, especially Arie van der Ploeg, Mathew Stagner, Luisiana Melendez, Dennis Lacewell, and Luis Soria for their thorough examination and insightful comments. In addition, we would like to acknowledge our colleagues at UChicago Impact for reviewing our report, including Elliot Ransom, Alex Seeskin, Molly Quish, and John Gasko. They helped us think about the ways in which this research would be most useful to practitioners. We are indebted to our colleagues at UChicago CCSR, who gave us encouragement and advice throughout, especially Elaine Allensworth, Jenny Nagaoka, Marisa de la Torre, and Rachel Levenstein. In addition, we would like to thank Todd Rosenkranz for preparing the data for analysis and Stuart Luppescu for his assistance with survey measures and his close read of the report. Special thanks to research assistant Anastasia Ovtcharova for her help, as well as Valerie Michelman and Matthew Holsapple for their valuable feedback as technical readers. Our communications team—Emily Krone, Bronwyn McDaniel, and Jessica Puller—were instrumental in carrying this work forward.

This report was made possible through the generous support of Priscilla and Steve Kersten, Patricia O. Cox, and the Lewis-Sebring Family Foundation. We also gratefully recognize the Spencer Foundation, whose operating grants support the work of UChicago CCSR.

Finally, we would like to thank the district- and school-level administrators who facilitated the survey and the teachers and students throughout Illinois who have taken the time to share their thoughts through the 5Essentials surveys.

This report was produced by UChicago CCSR's publications and communications staff: Emily Krone, Director for Outreach and Communication; Bronwyn McDaniel, Senior Manager for Outreach and Communication; and Jessica Puller, Communications Specialist.

Graphic Design: Jeff Hall Design
Photography: Cover: Shutterstock; Cynthia Howe
Editing: Ann Lindner

06.2015/pdf/jh.design@rcn.com

Executive Summary

During the spring of 2013, teachers and students in nearly 4,000 Illinois schools participated in the 5Essentials survey, a confidential survey administered statewide. Students in grades 6–12 and all teachers had the opportunity to share their perspectives about their school; teachers provided their perspectives about their school's leadership, professional community, and family involvement, while students responded to questions about the school environment and instruction. Ninety percent of Illinois schools participated in the survey; 85 percent of schools had data on at least three of five essential supports.

In this report, we investigate student and teacher responses to this survey. We use the framework of the five essential supports[1] to guide these analyses. These constructs are effective leaders, collaborative teachers, involved families, supportive environment, and ambitious instruction. Studies undertaken in schools and districts across the United States confirm that these specific domains are related to improving student outcomes.[2] In addition, previous research conducted by the University of Chicago Consortium on Chicago School Research (UChicago CCSR) in Chicago Public Schools (CPS)[3] found that schools strong in the five essential supports were much more likely than schools weak in these areas to see improvements in students' learning gains.

Because the survey was taken by students in grades 6-12, schools serving students in grades K–5 only contain teacher survey responses. For these schools, two of the 5Essentials that are made up entirely of student survey responses are missing—supportive environment and ambitious instruction. Thus K–5 schools received results for three of the five essential supports.

In this report, we address two overarching research questions: (1) How does strength and weakness on the five essential supports vary according to urbanicity, size of school, and socioeconomic characteristics of school communities? and (2) Are the five essential supports related to student outcomes including attendance rates, test scores, and graduation rates?

We caution that this is only a first look at the essential supports throughout Illinois. Because we relied on only one year of survey data and student outcomes prior to and simultaneous with the survey, we cannot make any conclusions about causal effects on student outcomes.

Key Findings

Strength in the five essential supports varies by urbanicity, school size, and socioeconomic conditions of the schools.

- Urban[4] and suburban schools were most likely to be strong in at least three essentials; rural schools were least likely.

---

1. Throughout this report, we will use *"five essential supports"* to refer to the framework and *"5Essentials"* to refer to the surveys used to measure the framework.
2. Goddard, Goddard, & Tschannen-Moran (2007); Hoy et al. (2006); Leithwood & Louis (Eds.), 2012; Sheldon & Epstein (2005); Wenglinsky (2000). Also see box on pg.8 *Evidence from Outside of Chicago That These Organizational Conditions Are Related to School Improvement*
3. Bryk, Sebring, Allensworth, Luppescu, & Easton (2010).
4. Urban includes all schools in Illinois classified as urban by the National Center for Education Statistics (NCES), including Chicago. See box *Defining Urbanicity* on p.13 for more information.

- In general, smaller schools are more likely to have strong essentials than larger schools, although the pattern is not as clear at the high school level.

- The more disadvantaged a school is socioeconomically, the less likely it is to have three or more strong essentials and the more likely it is to have three or more weak essentials. Although this relationship is true across all community areas in the state of Illinois, it is even more apparent in CPS.

Schools located in different community areas along the urban-rural continuum have strengths in different individual essentials.

- CPS schools are most likely to be strong in effective leaders, followed by schools in rural areas.

- Across Illinois, there is a similar proportion of schools strong in the collaborative teachers essential.

- The highest proportion of schools strong in involved families are located in suburban areas. Urban schools outside of Chicago, rural schools, town schools, and especially Chicago schools are less likely than suburban schools to be strong in involved families.

- Schools strongest in supportive environment are located in urban and suburban areas of the state.

- A higher proportion of schools in CPS is strong in ambitious instruction compared to schools located in other community areas across the state.

These findings echo prior research which suggests that schools in different locations face diverse challenges.

Being strong in the five essential supports is positively related to a number of student outcomes.

- For elementary and middle schools,[5] strength in the five essentials is related to attendance rate changes and to both math and reading gains on the ISAT, as well as to average ISAT scores and average attendance rates.

- For high schools, strength in the five essentials is related to attendance rate changes, as well as to average ACT scores, graduation rates, and attendance levels—although the relationships tend to be minimal, except for CPS where they are fairly substantial.

The associations between the essential supports and student outcomes varied from modest to substantial.

The findings of this preliminary investigation are encouraging—schools strong in the five essential supports are more likely to have better student outcomes. However, more work needs to be done to understand these relationships.

---

5 For purposes of this report, elementary and middle schools are those serving students in eighth grade and lower.

Introduction

Whole system change, we have learned, is not a kind of magic. It involves and absolutely requires individual and collective acts of investment in an inspirational vision and a coherent set of actions that build everyone's capability and keep everyone learning as they continue to move forward. —Hargreaves and Fullan, 2012[6]

High profile and sometimes expensive policies and practices aimed at improving student outcomes have been implemented in recent decades—accountability requirements, Teach for America, teacher evaluation, charter schools, and closing low-performing schools, to name a few. While each of these policies and programs may offer particular benefits, none provide holistic, clear guidance to school leaders, teachers, and parents about the health of their school organizations for promoting student engagement and learning.

A growing understanding is emerging, however, of the school organizational characteristics related to improved student learning. Based on longitudinal studies in Chicago, researchers at the University of Chicago Consortium on Chicago School Research (UChicago CCSR) have identified the significance of five essential supports for improving student performance.[7] The five essential supports framework encompasses effective leaders, collaborative teachers, involved families, a supportive environment for students, and ambitious instruction.[8] The Chicago studies showed that schools relatively strong in these domains were much more likely than schools relatively weak in these areas to see improvements in students' attendance and learning gains.[9] In addition, studies undertaken in schools and districts across the United States show a significant relationship between these five domains and improving student outcomes (**See box on p.8** *Evidence from Outside of Chicago...*).

To measure the five essential supports in schools, UChicago CCSR has relied on surveys of students and teachers. Because these surveys proved to be valid instruments[10] for measuring the five essential supports in Chicago schools, the Illinois State Board of Education (ISBE) selected UChicago Impact,[11] after a competitive bidding process, to conduct a statewide survey of students and teachers in 2013.[12]

---

6 Hargreaves & Fullan (2012).
7 Bryk et al. (2010).
8 These labels have changed over time. This report uses the labels from the current 5Essentials Survey. In the original study, these concepts were called Leadership as the Driver for Change, Professional Capacity, Parent-Community Ties, Student-Centered Learning Climate, and Instructional Guidance.
9 Bryk et al. (2010); Sebastian & Allensworth (2012).
10 See Bryk et al. 2010, Chapter 3, and Table A.5: Reliabilities of All Survey Measures Used to Construct the Essential Supports, in the Appendix.
11 UChicago Impact (2011, July 1).
12 In 2011, the Illinois State Legislature passed a law requiring school districts to administer a survey of learning conditions at least biennially starting in school year 2012-13 (105 ILCS 5/2-3.153). In 2012, legislation passed modifying the state school report card to include, *"Two or more indicators from any school climate survey developed by the State and administered pursuant to Section 2-3.153 of this Code."* (105 ILCS 5/10-17a). In 2012, in response to these requirements and with Race to the Top funding, ISBE put forth a Request for Sealed Proposals to develop the survey of learning conditions. Through a competitive bidding process, the University of Chicago, with its 5Essentials tool, was selected as the winning bidder.

The state of Illinois was motivated to offer the survey because it wanted to provide schools and communities data beyond test scores that could help them identify ways to improve their schools. Thus, in 2011 the legislature passed a law requiring the Illinois State Board of Education (ISBE) to *"select for statewide administration an instrument to provide feedback from, at a minimum, students in grades 6 through 12 and teachers on the instructional environment within a school."*[13] Note that the purpose of the survey was to provide a report with results to local schools, which they could use for planning and action. *"As educators, we have long understood that test scores alone do not represent the full scope of school life and learning,"* said State Superintendent of Education Christopher A. Koch. *"The Illinois 5Essentials Survey will finally help us paint that fuller picture of learning conditions and guide local and state improvement initiatives…"*[14]

For the first time, the Illinois 5Essentials survey makes it possible to characterize how relatively strong or relatively weak the five essential support practices are in diverse school contexts—in Chicago, smaller cities, suburbs, towns, and rural areas. Furthermore, the statewide survey responses allow researchers to explore for Illinois public schools whether strength in the essential support practices is related to improvement in student outcomes.

Therefore, the purpose of this study is to expand stakeholders' understanding of the five essential supports in K–12 schools and how they may vary among different types of schools and community contexts. In particular, we want to establish whether the five essential supports are related to student outcomes in Illinois schools. Of equal importance, we want to provide an overall profile of Illinois schools on the five essential supports for policymakers, educators, parents, and other stakeholders. This, in turn, will help to illuminate the kinds of schools that show robust organizational features (as reported by their teachers and students) versus those that exhibit organizational weaknesses. Hence, this statewide study is a complement to the individual reports that schools receive.

We address two overarching research questions for this study:

1 How does strength and weakness on the five essential supports vary according to urbanicity, size of school, and socioeconomic characteristics of school communities?

2 Are the five essential supports related to student outcomes including attendance rates, test scores, and graduation rates?

Consistent with the title of this report, we view this as a first step in understanding the five essential supports across Illinois schools. We rely primarily on a single year of survey data (2013) and the attendance rates, test scores, and graduation rates for 2011–13. In the future, we will request additional years of data to further investigate our research questions.

In Chapter 1, we define the five essential supports, review the research undergirding the supports, and describe the Illinois surveys. In Chapter 2, we explore how the five essential supports vary by urbanicity, school size, and community socioeconomic characteristics. In Chapter 3, we delve into the relationships between essential support practices and student outcomes. Finally, in Chapter 4, we offer an interpretation of what the five essential supports mean for practice.

---

[13] Illinois State Board of Education (n.d.a).
[14] Illinois State Board of Education News (2013, January 30).

CHAPTER 1

Exploring the Five Essential Supports in Illinois Schools

Origins of the Five Essential Supports

The framework and surveys have their roots in Chicago, where in the 1990s educators asked a simple question: Why were some elementary schools improving dramatically, while others remained stagnant? During a six-year period, from 1990 to 1996, there were 118 schools out of 477 that had increased the percentage of their students meeting national norms in reading, from 22 to 37 percent. At the same time, there were another 118 elementary schools where the trend was essentially flat—24 percent met national norms at the beginning and at the end of the six-year period. Together, these two sets of diverging schools served more than 150,000 students.[15]

Faced with these widely divergent sets of outcomes, the CPS superintendent invited UChicago CCSR researchers to join educators and school reformers in Chicago to begin developing a systemwide guide for school improvement. These early discussions with educators, examination of national research, pilot surveys, and field studies of schools led to the first articulation of the framework of the five essential supports for school improvement (**see Figure 1**). The framework served as both a clinical guide for practitioners and as a theoretical guide for developing surveys to measure each component.

The framework asserts that effective leadership, acting as a catalyst, is the first essential support for school improvement. The leader must stimulate and nourish the development of four additional core organizational supports: collaborative teachers, involved families, supportive environment, and ambitious instruction. While each of these supports is important on its own, the value of these supports lies in their integration and mutual reinforcement. For example, in schools where teachers and other staff get to know their students individually and provide social and academic supports (or, in the language of the framework, provide a supportive environment), it is more likely that students will rise to the high expectations of ambitious instruction.[16]

The five essential supports reflect the vital connection between a school's organization and what happens in the classroom. While the teacher in his/her own classroom has the most direct responsibility for raising student achievement, the broader school organization

FIGURE 1
Framework of the Five Essential Supports

---

15 Bryk et al. (2010).
16 Bryk et al. (2010).

also must be structured in a way that supports teachers in their efforts to enhance students' learning.[17] A contemporary example of this is that teachers who incorporate nonfiction literature into their curriculum and/or integrate laptops or tablets need time and a structure for organizing this work. They may need common planning time with their colleagues, schedules for implementing new lessons, professional development, opportunities for feedback, and a way to monitor progress. This all works best when there is strong trust among the adults, and when they believe it is safe to try new and innovative ideas.[18] Without such organizational support, there is little coordination, and too much falls on the individual teacher; improvement efforts are likely to misfire. How successful teachers are in strengthening their instruction depends on the robustness of the essential support practices in the school. We describe each of these below.

Effective Leaders

Effective leadership requires taking a strategic approach toward enhancing performance of the four other domains, while simultaneously nurturing the social relationships embedded in the everyday work of the school. Leaders advance their objectives, particularly with respect to improving instruction, while at the same time seeking to develop supportive followers for change. In the process, they cultivate other leaders—teachers, parents, and community members—who can take responsibility for and help expand the reach of improvement efforts.

Collaborative Teachers

This construct encompasses the quality of the human resources recruited and maintained in a school, the quality of ongoing professional development focused on local improvement efforts, the base beliefs and values that reflect teacher responsibility for change, and the presence of a school-based professional community focused on the core problems of improving teaching and learning. The four elements of collaborative teachers are mutually reinforcing and together promote both individual and collective growth. A recent example of this is a school that trained teachers to collaborate. Together the teachers defined collaboration; they created structures and routines to facilitate collaboration; and they monitored whether they were working effectively together. Specifically, they made sure that at all grade-level meetings they discussed new lessons, the students who were having difficulties, and their ongoing analysis of the quality of student work.

Involved Families

School staff reach out to families and the community to engage them in the processes of strengthening student learning. Staff view parents or guardians as partners in their children's learning and report that they feel respected by those parents. Examples of this can range from bringing parents of preschool and primary grade children together for activities to grandparents' clubs that come to school to read with students.

Supportive Environment

A safe and orderly environment that is conducive to academic work is critical to a supportive environment. Clear, fair, and consistently enforced expectations for student behavior ensure that students receive maximum instructional time. Teachers must hold students to high expectations of academic achievement while also providing considerable individual attention and support for students. An example of a systematic way of providing such support is to assess students frequently and use the information both to adjust instruction and to remediate gaps in students' learning.

Ambitious Instruction

It is widely agreed that to prepare students for further schooling, specialized work, and responsible civic participation, teachers must move beyond the basic skills and ask students to do intellectually challenging work. Such learning tasks require students to organize and plan their work, monitor their progress, and oftentimes work in teams. Modern examples of this are writing poetry, building robots, creating math puzzles, and conducting scientific experiments.

---

[17] Bryk et al. (2010).
[18] Bryk et al. (2010).

The five essentials framework also posits that leadership and the other four core supports exist within a broader context of a climate of mutual trust. Trust is a key social resource for school improvement. The original work in Chicago found that without a strong base of trust, it is nearly impossible to achieve the level of communication and collaboration needed for getting work done. The essential supports are most likely to develop in schools where mutual trust suffuses the working relationships across the school community. At the same time, we recognize the substantial role played by the local community in a school's capacity to improve. Stresses of poverty, crime, and other social problems make it more challenging to operate a school. The opposite also is true. Social resources like churches and voluntary organizations can contribute positively to how a school functions.[19]

Linking the Five Essential Supports to Improvements in Chicago: The Original Study[20]

To determine whether the essential supports were related to improvements in learning outcomes, UChicago CCSR developed and administered teacher and student surveys that measured relevant practices in elementary and middle schools since the 1990s. Survey items were combined into scales or measures of particular constructs, such as the *"quality of professional development."* Outcome measures were created from annual individual student test scores in reading and mathematics on the Iowa Tests of Basic Skills (ITBS). From the test scores, researchers constructed an academic productivity profile for each school that determined whether students who attended each school were making learning gains each year and whether those gains were increasing between the 1990–91 and 1995–96 school years.[21] Together, the test scores and the survey data permitted UChicago CCSR to test the hypothesis that schools stronger in the essential support practices would be more likely to show improving learning gains in reading and mathematics than schools where the essential support practices were weak.

The original study found that strength in any single essential support elevated the probability of improvement in learning gains in both reading and mathematics. For example, the probability of substantial improvement in math learning gains was seven times higher among elementary and middle schools with strong leadership than among schools with weak leadership (42 percent compared to 6 percent). Researchers also went on to examine the cumulative effects associated with being strong in three to five essentials simultaneously. Elementary and middle schools strong in most supports were about 10 times more likely than schools weak in most supports to show substantial gains in both reading and mathematics. Not a single school weak in three or more supports showed substantial improvements in mathematics. Furthermore, a material weakness in only one support that continued for three years seemed to undermine reform efforts, as almost none of the schools with a sustained weakness in one support showed improvements.[22]

It is worth remembering that schools were classified as relatively strong or relatively weak on an essential based on students' and teachers' responses to the survey questions about their school. The juxtaposition of survey responses with students' learning gains in the same schools indicates that they are empirically linked. Schools that students and teachers indicate are strong also show higher probabilities of improvement. This makes sense as students and teachers *"live"* in their school every day and thus can accurately capture the school's organizational features.[23]

Returning to Chicago educators' original question about why some elementary schools improved and others did not, these results provided evidence that those schools that made steady progress were more likely to be robust school organizations. They were more likely to have strong essential support practices, which was one thing that differentiated them from the stagnating schools. This held true for most schools in the study that were in racially isolated, poor communities as well as moderate income, racially integrated schools. In addition, a replication analysis based on data collected from 1997-2005 revealed mostly similar findings.

---

19 Bryk et al. (2010).
20 Bryk et al. (2010).
21 Bryk et al. (2010).
22 Bryk et al. (2010).
23 Bryk et al. (2010), Appendix G.

Subsequent Findings Regarding High Schools

In 2012, two UChicago CCSR researchers expanded on the original elementary school findings, teasing out the ways in which leadership is related to the other essential support practices in Chicago high schools.[24] Comparing high schools, the authors found that differences in instruction and student achievement were associated with principal leadership only via the learning climate. This suggests that in high schools, establishing a safe, college-focused climate may be the most important leadership function for promoting achievement schoolwide.

Evidence from Outside of Chicago That These Organizational Conditions Are Related to School Improvement

Though the validation work on the framework occurred in Chicago, the framework was originally developed using evidence from across the country on the important factors for school improvement. There is considerable evidence from other scholars who have done studies in multiple contexts that these individual learning conditions are related to improved student outcomes. The following is a brief summary of this evidence:

Effective Leaders: Many studies have shown that school leaders have a positive and significant, albeit indirect, relationship with student achievement. This relationship works through other organizational conditions including the school environment or culture, as well as through teacher professional community.[A] In the largest, most recent national study on school leadership, researchers looking at data from nine states, 44 school districts, and 138 schools found that "school leaders have an impact on student achievement primarily through their influence on teachers' motivation and working conditions."[B] Furthermore, in a meta-analysis of leadership studies, researchers found that instructional leadership behaviors had the largest indirect relationship with student outcomes.[C] Certain principal instructional leadership tasks, such as time spent evaluating and coaching teachers and developing the school's educational program, are more closely related to improving student outcomes than others tasks, according to recent studies done in Massachusetts, Miami, and Florida.[D]

Collaborative Teachers: Researchers have found an association between schools with higher levels of collaboration among teachers who feel collectively responsible for all students in the school and significantly higher achievement.[E] In studies using data from Massachusetts and a large Midwestern urban district, researchers discovered an association between teachers working closely together to share ideas and resources across classrooms and student learning.[F] Similarly, in a national study undertaken in a variety of school contexts, researchers found a significantly positive relationship between teachers' collective sense of responsibility for students' learning and classroom instructional practices that are student centered and focused.[G]

A Louis et al. (2010); Hallinger & Heck (1996); Hallinger & Heck (1998); Hallinger & Heck (2010); Witziers, Bosker, & Krüger (2003); Robinson, Lloyd, & Rowe (2008).
B Leithwood & Louis (2012).
C Robinson et al. (2008).
D Grissom & Loeb (2011); Grissom, Loeb, & Master (2013); Johnson, Kraft, & Papay (2012).
E Louis et al. (2010); Wahlstrom & Louis (2008).
F Goddard, Goddard, & Tschannen-Moran (2007); Johnson et al. (2012).
G Wahlstrom & Louis (2008).

---

24 Sebastian & Allensworth (2012).

EVIDENCE FROM OUTSIDE OF CHICAGO...*CONTINUED*

Involved Families: Strong family and community involvement is significantly and positively related to student achievement.[H] One study found a significant relationship between school family partnership programs emphasizing teacher and parent collaboration and frequent communication between teachers and parents and academic achievement of students.[I] A different study found that in schools with higher levels of trust between teachers and families, student achievement in math and reading was higher.[J]

Supportive Environment: Researchers posit that students learn best in schools that are safe, orderly, and supportive.[K] For example, in schools where staff have high expectations for student learning and drive students to achieve at their greatest potential, researchers have found a positive relationship with student learning gains.[L] A study done in Ohio shows that teachers, students, parents, and administrators having high expectations and believing students can reach their goals is positively related to student learning outcomes.[M]

Ambitious Instruction: Several researchers have found a significant relationship between students exposed to clear, coherent, and high quality instruction and higher learning outcomes.[N] For example, a researcher investigating national student NAEP scores in mathematics found that in classrooms where teachers stress higher-order thinking and use hands-on learning techniques, students' math scores are higher.[O] Furthermore, in a study looking at data from classroom observations from a sample of New York City English/language arts teachers, researchers found that, on average, teachers who broke down the specific components of literary analysis, reading comprehension, and writing were more likely to improve student test scores compared to peers who did not use these strategies.[P]

Most researchers have examined these conditions either individually or as a small subset of related variables. The five essentials framework is unique in that it tests all of these different organizational factors at once. The power of the five essentials framework is in the synergy created by all five essential supports and how they work together.

[H] Sheldon & Epstein (2005); Forsyth, Barnes, & Adams (2006).
[I] Jeynes (2012).
[J] Goddard, Tschannen-Moran, & Hoy (2001).
[K] Robers, Kemp, & Truman (2013); Bowen & Bowen (1999); Klem & Connell (2004).
[L] Hoy, Tarter, & Hoy (2006); Hardré, Sullivan, & Crowson (2009).
[M] Hoy et al. (2006); Goddard, Sweetland, & Hoy (2000).
[N] Reys, Reys, Lapan, Holliday, & Wasman (2003); Ginsburg-Block & Fantuzzo (1998); Stronge, Ward, Tucker, & Hindman (2007); Matsumura, Slater, & Crosson (2008).
[O] Wenglinsky (2000).
[P] Grossman et al. (2010).

Overview of the Illinois Survey

During spring of 2013, teachers and students in nearly 4,000 Illinois schools participated in the confidential, statewide 5Essentials survey. The survey provided students in grades 6–12 and all teachers the opportunity to share their perspectives about their school.[25] A few months after taking the survey, each Illinois school received summary statistics of its own survey results, and in subsequent years schools received individual school reports (see https://illinois.5-essentials.org/2014_public/ and https://cps.5-essentials.org/2014/).

The vast majority of Illinois schools took part in the 5Essentials survey in 2013. The number and percentage of schools, teachers, and students in the data we are using for this report are as follows:

- **Schools**—3,684 or 85 percent of Illinois schools
- **Teachers**—104,270, or 68 percent of Illinois teachers
- **Students**—750,326, or 68 percent of Illinois students

UChicago CCSR and UChicago Impact in Relation to the 5Essentials Surveys

Between 1991 and 2009, UChicago CCSR both developed and administered the 5Essentials teacher and student surveys in the CPS.[26] In 2008, the University of Chicago created the Urban Education Institute (UChicago UEI), of which UChicago CCSR became the research arm. The university established UChicago Impact as part of UChicago UEI in 2011 to continue to develop and provide tools and support services for strengthening teaching, learning, and school improvement, including the 5Essentials survey, the STEP early literacy assessment, and the 6to16 college readiness curriculum. It now administers the 5Essentials survey in Chicago, the state of Illinois, and other jurisdictions in the United States. Although UChicago Impact staff administer the surveys, researchers at UChicago CCSR continue to develop and hone the 5Essential survey questions (including those in 2013), and create scales and measures. Therefore, although the two units are independent, they do collaborate on the 5Essentials survey.

Survey Items and Measures

In the surveys, teachers and students respond to individual questions that capture particular concepts. **Figure 2** shows an example. On the right, you can see the five items that students answered. For each student, researchers combine these items to obtain a score for the overall measure—in this case, student-teacher trust.[27] In turn, this measure is combined with safety and academic personalism, as well as peer support for academic work and academic press for students in the middle grades and schoolwide future orientation and expectations for post-secondary education for high schools, to create a score for one of the five essentials—supportive environment. **See Appendix A Table A.2** for correlations among the essential supports, **Appendix A Table A.5** for information about reliability, and **see Appendix B** for information about the individual survey items.

In all, there are 22 measures that capture the five essential supports. (**See box *5Essential Survey Measures*.**) Note that each measure is based on either teachers' or students' responses, and some pertain to elementary or middle schools only, while others are asked of high school teachers or students only.

K-5 Schools Have Data on Three of the Five Essentials

Grade configuration of schools matters because it affects whether there are student responses on the 5Essential surveys. Because student surveys are given to students in grades 6–12, schools serving students in grades K–5 do not have any student responses; teachers are the sole informants for these schools. Therefore, because two of the essentials are based mostly or solely on student measures, K–5 schools are missing data for ambitious instruction and supportive environment. In addition, K–5 schools do not have one of the three measures that constitute the involved families essential—Human and

---

25 ISBE also offered schools a voluntary parent survey, which is not formally part of the 5Essentials survey system.

26 The results of the 5Essentials surveys in CPS have been public since 2011. In 2014, CPS began using the 5Essential surveys as part of their accountability framework. Because of the number of years that CPS has been taking the 5Essentials surveys, teachers, administrators, and families are more familiar with the surveys and are facing different levels of accountability tied to the survey results, compared to other schools in the state.

27 For an explanation of scoring, see http://help.5-essentials.org/customer/portal/articles/94413-how-scores-are-calculated.

FIGURE 2

Survey Items Form Measures; Measures Form Essentials

Supportive Environment

Measures
- Peer Support for Academic Work (MS)
- Academic Press (MS)
- School-Wide Future Orientation (HS)
- Expectations for Post-Secondary Education (HS)
- Academic Personalism
- Student-Teacher Trust
- Safety

Items
- My teachers always keep their promises.
- I feel safe and comfortable with my teachers at this school.
- My teachers always listen to student's ideas.
- When my teachers tell me not to do something I know they have a good reason.
- My teachers treat me with respect.

5Essentials Survey Measures

Ambitious Instruction
- Course Clarity (S)
- English/Language Arts Instruction (S)
- Math Instruction (S)
- Quality of Student Discussion (S)

Effective Leaders
- Teacher Influence (T)
- Principal Instructional Leadership (T)
- Program Coherence (T)
- Teacher–Principal Trust (T)

Collaborative Teachers
- Collective Responsibility (T)
- Quality Professional Development (T)
- School Commitment (T)
- Teacher–Teacher Trust (T)

Involved Families
- Human and Social Resources in the Community (S)
- Teacher Outreach to Parents (T)
- Teacher–Parent Trust (T)

Supportive Environment
- Peer Support for Academic Work (Elem/Middle) (S)
- Academic Personalism (S)
- Academic Press (Elem/Middle) (S)
- Safety (S)
- Student–Teacher Trust (S)
- School-Wide Future Orientation (HS) (S)
- Expectations for Post-Secondary Education (HS) (T)

(S) Student Measure
(T) Teacher Measure

Social Resources in the Community, which is also a student measure. For these reasons, we often display findings separately for K–5 schools that have the *"3Essential Supports"* of effective leaders, collaborative teachers, and the teacher measures for involved families.

The availability of valid survey data for K–5 schools primarily affects schools outside of Chicago. **Table 1** shows that while there are K–8 schools throughout the state, schools serving grades K–5 and 6-8 with valid survey data are primarily found outside of CPS.

TABLE 1

Distribution of Schools with Valid 5Essentials Survey Data by Grade Configuration

	Outside of CPS	CPS	Total
K–5	1242	24	1266
K–8	827	445	1272
6–8	491	9	500
9–12	535	111	646
Total	**3095**	**589**	**3684**

Note: Valid data refers to schools that have information on at least three essential supports.

CHAPTER 2

How the Essential Supports Vary across Communities, School Types

In this section, we examine how the five essential supports differ across community contexts and types of schools in Illinois. In particular, we focus on varying degrees of urbanicity (urban, suburban, town, rural), school size (student enrollment), and student and community socioeconomic disadvantage.

To do this analysis, we placed schools into quartiles based on the average of each of their essential scores. This was done separately for elementary/middle schools and for high schools. We defined schools with the highest scores on the survey on each of the 5Essentials (top 25 percent) as the strongest on that essential and the schools with the lowest scores on the survey in each essential (bottom 25 percent) as the weakest. Any schools with scores that fell in the middle half are referred to as "typical."[28] We go on to compare schools with different characteristics and in varying contexts on whether they have three or more strong essentials, have three or more weak essentials, or are typical. This analysis was done separately for elementary/middle schools and for high schools because of the different survey measures given to students and teachers by grade levels (**See box *5Essentials Survey Measures***).[29]

Distribution of the Five Essential Supports by Urbanicity

We placed schools into categories based on their community type: urban, suburban, town, or rural. Because Chicago is so much larger than the other urban districts, we separate it out for our analyses.[30] **See box *Defining Urbanicity*** for definitions of these categories.

The largest group of schools in our analysis are in suburban communities (37 percent), followed by 24 percent of schools in rural communities, 16 percent in

Defining Urbanicity

We used community classifications from the National Center for Education Statistics (NCES) database. Schools are classified into the following community types: city, suburb, town, and rural. In the NCES database, these community types are further denoted by size (small, mid-size, large) and distance (fringe, distant, remote). However, for the purpose of our analysis, we chose to use the general community classifications described in more detail below.

Urban School: A school in an urbanized area (territory with at least 50,000 residents) that is the principal city in a core-based statistical area. The principal cities in Illinois are Chicago, Arlington Heights, Bloomington, Bradley, Champaign, Danville, Decatur, Des Plaines, Elgin, Evanston, Hoffman Estates, Joliet, Kankakee, Moline, Naperville, Normal, Peoria, Plainfield, Rock Island, Rockford, Schaumburg, Skokie, Springfield, and Urbana.

Suburban School: A school in an urbanized area outside a principal city.

Town School: A school in a territory with 2,500–50,000 residents.

Rural School: A school in a territory with fewer than 2,500 residents.

---

[28] These are not quite the same as the benchmarked strong and weak indicators on the Illinois State Board of Education (ISBE) school report cards; but for the purpose of this report, readers can think of *"strong"* as being in the highest category on the school reports and *"weak"* as being in the lowest category.

[29] It is important to note that our analysis for this section is not the same as the analysis done in the original study in Chicago, and is therefore not a replication of that study.

[30] Total student enrollment for CPS in the 2012-13 school year was 403,593, for instance, whereas total enrollment for the second largest urban district in Illinois, Elgin Area School District (SD U-46), was 40,314.

Chicago, 13 percent in towns, and 10 percent in urban centers beyond Chicago. Since the vast majority of Illinois schools participated in the 5Essentials surveys, these proportions are similar to those for all Illinois schools. **(See Appendix Table A.1** for the distribution of schools with survey data by community location.)

Previous research has shown that schools and students in varying community contexts face different kinds of challenges. For example, one study using a nationally representative dataset showed that, in general, parents in urban and suburban settings tend to have higher educational expectations for their children than parents in rural contexts, but rural students have access to more social capital (such as their parents knowing their own friends' parents) than students in urban contexts. On average, rural students are also less likely to have access to and/or take higher level courses than their urban and suburban counterparts.[31] Other researchers found inequalities in the level of economic resources available to students by context; inner city and rural students have access to fewer resources than students in suburban schools.[32] How do these dynamics play out in Illinois?

> At the elementary/middle school level, a slightly higher proportion of schools located in urban areas are strong in three or more essentials, although CPS schools are also more likely to be weak. We see a starker contrast at the high school level, with a higher proportion of schools located in urban and suburban areas strong in at least three essentials, but also a higher proportion of weak urban schools.

Elementary/middle schools located in rural areas and towns are less likely to be strong in the essentials than schools located in urban regions. Chicago elementary/middle schools, on the other hand, differ from elementary/middle schools in other types of communities in that they are more likely to have three or more weak essential supports, but also more likely to have three or more strong essentials **(see Figure 3)**.

The picture becomes more complicated at the high school level. Suburban high schools are the most likely to be strong in the essential supports compared to high schools in other community locations across the state. Urban schools (including Chicago) are the most likely to be weak. At the same time, rural high schools are the least likely to be either strong or weak, with more schools falling into the middle range.

Examining strength in all five essentials at once obscures some differences by urbanicity in the strength of particular essentials (i.e., effective leadership or family involvement). **Figure 4** shows that strength or weakness on each of the supports is related to the type of community in which the school is located.

CPS has the largest percentage of schools that fall into the top quartile on three of the essential supports: effective leaders, collaborative teachers, and ambitious instruction **(see Figure 4)**. However, CPS has the smallest percentage of schools that fall into the top quartile in family involvement. One possible reason why Chicago schools lag so far behind in the family essential compared to schools in other locations may be that one of the three measures within the involved families essential is a measure of the community's social capital—or what we call human and social resources in the community. The questions in this measure ask students about their community and neighborhood connections, trust of adults in the community, and safety in the community. A high level of crime and violence in some Chicago neighborhoods may undermine building social capital within these neighborhoods.

Schools in suburban areas, on the other hand, are the most likely to fall into the top quartile on family involvement compared to schools located in other contexts. We see less variation across the state in terms of the collaborative teachers essential. Urban and suburban communities have a much higher proportion of schools strong in instruction, compared to schools in towns and rural areas. However, it would be a mistake to exaggerate the disadvantages rural schools face: Outside of CPS, they are the most likely to be strong in effective leaders.

---

31 Byun, Meece, & Irvin (2012). This study used National Education Longitudinal Study (NELS) data to investigate differences by community location on student postsecondary attainment.
32 Roscigno, Tomaskovic-Devey, & Crowley (2006). These authors used National Education Longitudinal Study (NELS) and Common Core of Data (CCD) to investigate educational resource inequality across spatial stratification as it relates to student educational outcomes.

FIGURE 3

Both Elem/Middle Schools and High Schools in Urban Areas Are More Likely to Be Strong in Three or More Essentials; Although a Higher Proportion of Urban High Schools Are Weak in Three or More Essentials

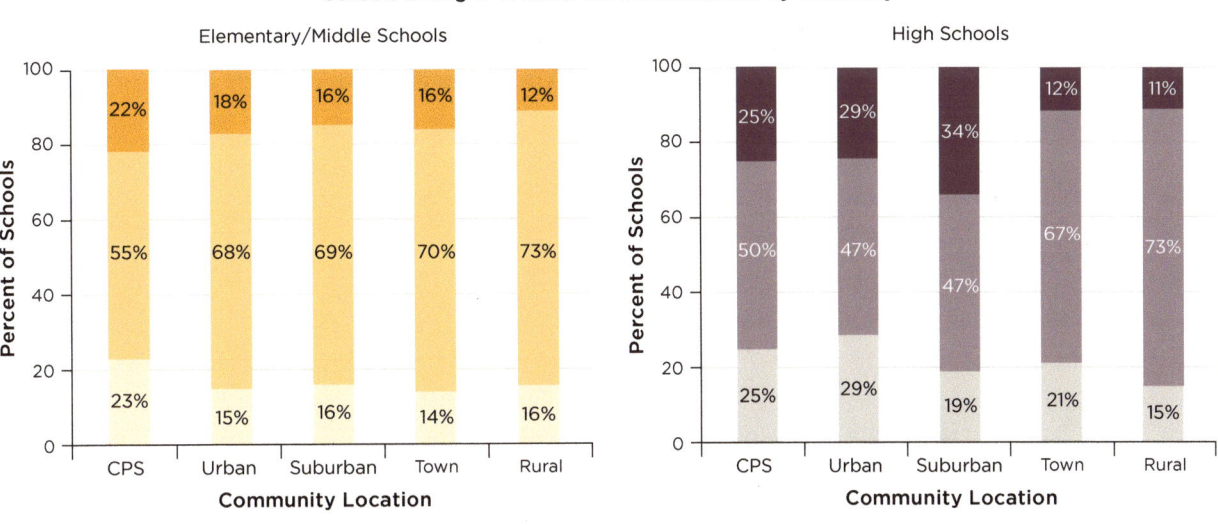

FIGURE 4

Urban and Suburban Communities Have a Much Higher Proportion of Schools Strong in Instruction, Compared to Schools in Towns and Rural Communities

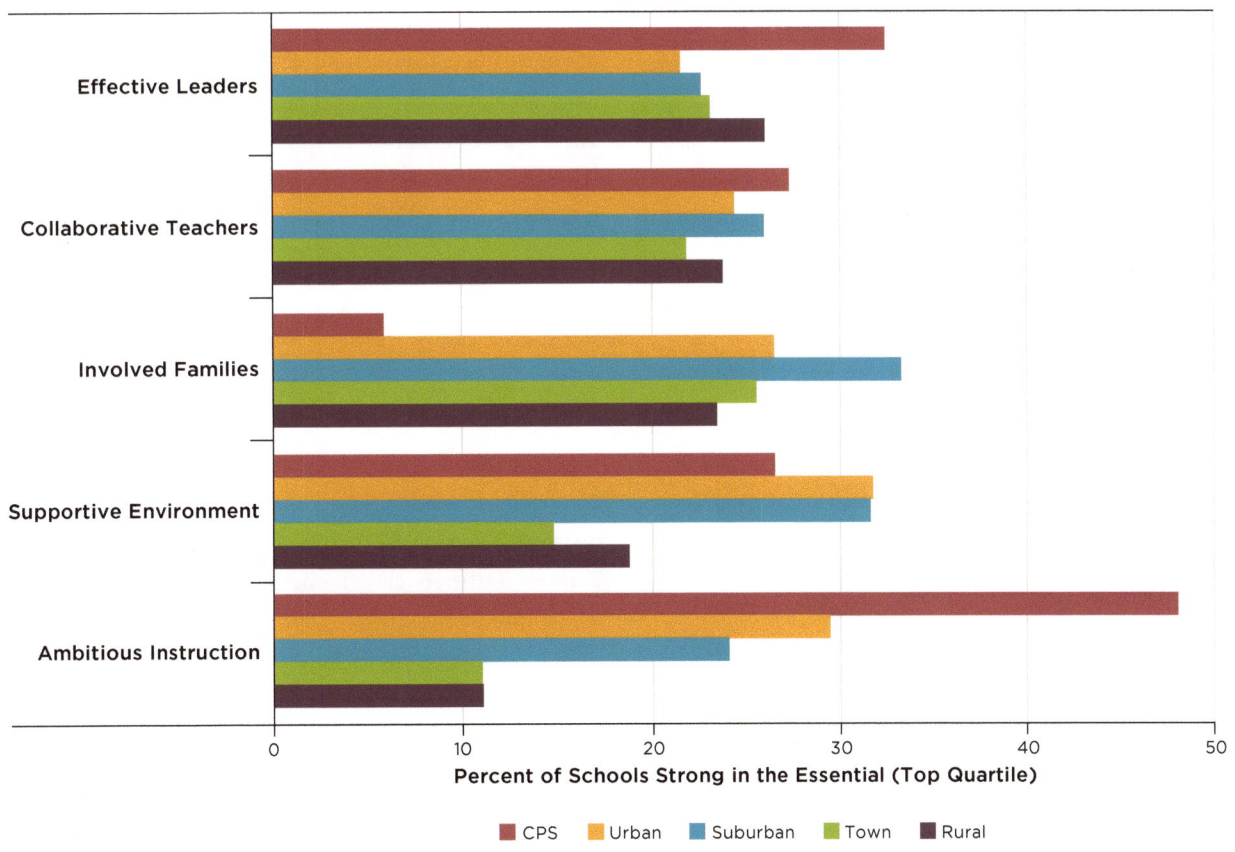

Note: This figure includes all schools with data on at least three of the five essentials data in the state. This figure combines elementary and high schools.

Chapter 2 | How the Five Essential Supports Vary across Communities and School Types

Distribution of the Five Essential Supports by School Size

Previous research has suggested that school size is important for school culture and organizational practices. The original Chicago study, for example, found that the five essential supports were more likely to be strong in smaller elementary schools than larger ones.[33] In other areas of the country, researchers found that the interpersonal dynamics within the schools are weaker in larger schools, as students are more likely to feel less connected to their school and to their teachers.[34] There is also evidence that students are more likely to benefit academically in smaller elementary schools than larger ones.[35]

However, the relationship between school size and interpersonal and organizational dynamics is not as straightforward at the high school level. In general, researchers have found that student connection and attachment to school is more difficult in larger high schools, but there appears to be a threshold where this dynamic is reversed—in high schools with student bodies larger than 1,000.[36] Authors of these studies speculate that in much larger high schools students have more access to high quality teachers with specialized subject matter expertise. Prior studies on high school size and student performance are mixed. Some studies, for example, show a relationship between small to mid-size high schools and higher student performance, engagement, and connectedness.[37] Also, researchers have found associations between smaller schools and learning gains and connectedness for socioeconomically disadvantaged student populations.[38] How do these distributions look across Illinois schools?

> A higher proportion of larger (≥600 students) elementary/middles schools are weak in 3 or more essentials, compared to smaller elementary/middle schools. The relationship between enrollment and strength in the five essentials is less clear at the high school level.

When we examine strength and weakness of the essential supports in relation to enrollment or size of elementary/middle schools in Illinois, we see some patterns (see **Figure 5**): Larger elementary schools (≥600 students) are more likely to be weak in three or more essentials, although the relationship between enrollment and strength in the five essentials is less clear for high schools.[39] An elementary/middle school's chances of being weak on the essential supports increase when school enrollment exceeds 600 students, going from around 23 to 39 percent. About 40 percent of elementary/middle schools with enrollments exceeding 1,000 students are weak on three or more essentials.

The pattern is more complex at the high school level. As shown in **Figure 5**, in general, larger high schools (>500) tend to have three or more weak essentials, but this pattern reverses after high schools reach an enrollment threshold of around 1,000 students. More specifically, 35 percent of high schools with enrollments between 700-999 are weak in at least three essentials, but only 27 percent of high schools with ≥1,000 students are weak in three essentials. The relationship between high school size and having at least three strong essentials, is less clear. Larger high schools (≥700 students) are more likely to be strong on the essential supports, compared to smaller high schools. High schools with enrollments between 500-699, on the other hand, are the least likely to be strong on three or more essentials. **See Appendix A Table A.3** for the distribution of school size for elementary/middle and high schools in Illinois.

Distribution of the Five Essential Supports by Student and Community Socioeconomic Disadvantage

Concerns about equity motivate us to examine the socioeconomic conditions of schools to see how these may be related to whether or not a school is a robust organization. In Illinois, the proportion of students in public schools who are considered low income climbed to 52 percent in 2014. This includes students whose families

---

33 Bryk et al. (2010).
34 Leithwood & Jantzi (2009).
35 Leithwood & Jantzi (2009).
36 Crosnoe, Johnson, & Elder (2004).
37 Leithwood & Jantzi (2009).
38 Leithwood & Jantzi (2009).
39 About 75 percent of Illinois schools with at least three of the five essentials are small or medium with respect to enrollment, serving fewer than 600 students. See Table A.2 in Appendix A for the distribution of schools by size.

FIGURE 5

A Higher Proportion of Larger (≥600 Students) Elementary/Middle Schools Are Weak in Three or More Essentials, Compared to Smaller Elementary/Middle Schools. The Relationship Between Enrollment and Strength in the Five Essentials Is Less Clear at the High School Level

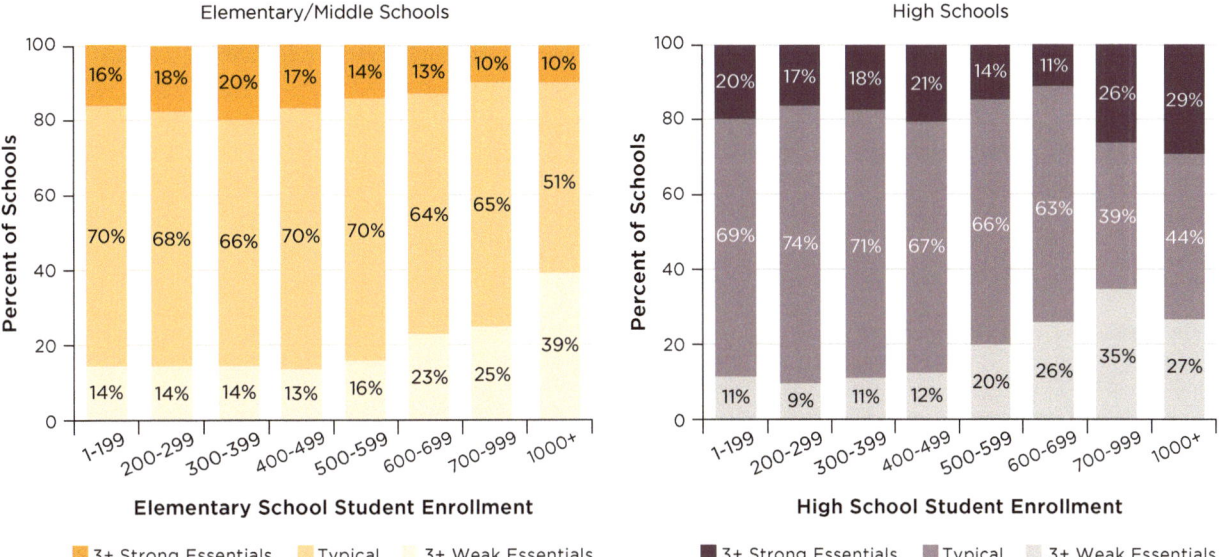

Note: The number in each of the columns represents the percentage of schools that fall into that category.

receive public aid, or are eligible for free or reduced-price lunch.⁴⁰ We present the analysis separately for CPS because the patterns of socioeconomic disadvantage are so different for schools in Chicago than they are for schools located in other community areas across the state. Close to 80 percent of schools in Chicago, for example, fall into the most disadvantaged category, compared to 30 percent of schools in cities outside of Chicago, 18 percent in suburban regions, 15 percent in towns, and 5 percent in rural contexts. **See Appendix A Table A.4.**

Schools located in socioeconomically disadvantaged communities are less likely to be strong in the essentials, compared to schools located in the least disadvantaged communities. The effect of socioeconomic disadvantage is stronger in Chicago than the rest of Illinois.

Measuring Socioeconomic Context of Schools

To measure socioeconomic disadvantage, we use a standardized scale combining information about the school and the surrounding area.^Q For the school, we use the percent of students eligible for free or reduced-priced lunch (averaged across the 2011-12 and 2012-13 school years, and obtained from the Common Core of Data). For the surrounding area, we obtained data from the 2007-11 American Community Survey (ACS) on the area's poverty rate and the percent of males 16 years or older that were jobless.

Q If districts have less than 1,000 students enrolled, the *"surrounding area"* was the district; otherwise, the *"surrounding area"* was the Census tract where the school was located.

---

40 Illinois State Board of Education (n.d.b).

Among schools outside of Chicago, 30 percent of the most disadvantaged schools have three or more weak essentials and only 8 percent have three or more strong essentials (see Figure 6). On the other hand, 24 percent of the least disadvantaged schools have three or more strong essentials and only 6 percent are weak in at least three. These findings are consistent with other research showing that schools serving more disadvantaged students face more challenges than schools with more affluent students.[41]

The relationship between socioeconomic disadvantage and the essentials is even more apparent in Chicago, where 54 percent of the least disadvantaged schools in CPS are strong in three or more essential supports and only 18 percent of the most disadvantaged schools are strong. The most disadvantaged schools in Chicago, on the other hand, are more likely to have three or more weak essentials. As Figure 6 shows, none of the least disadvantaged CPS schools have three or more weak essentials.

FIGURE 6

Disadvantaged Schools Are Less Likely to Be Strong On Three or More Essentials; The Effect of Socioeconomic Disadvantage is Stronger in Chicago Than the Rest of Illinois

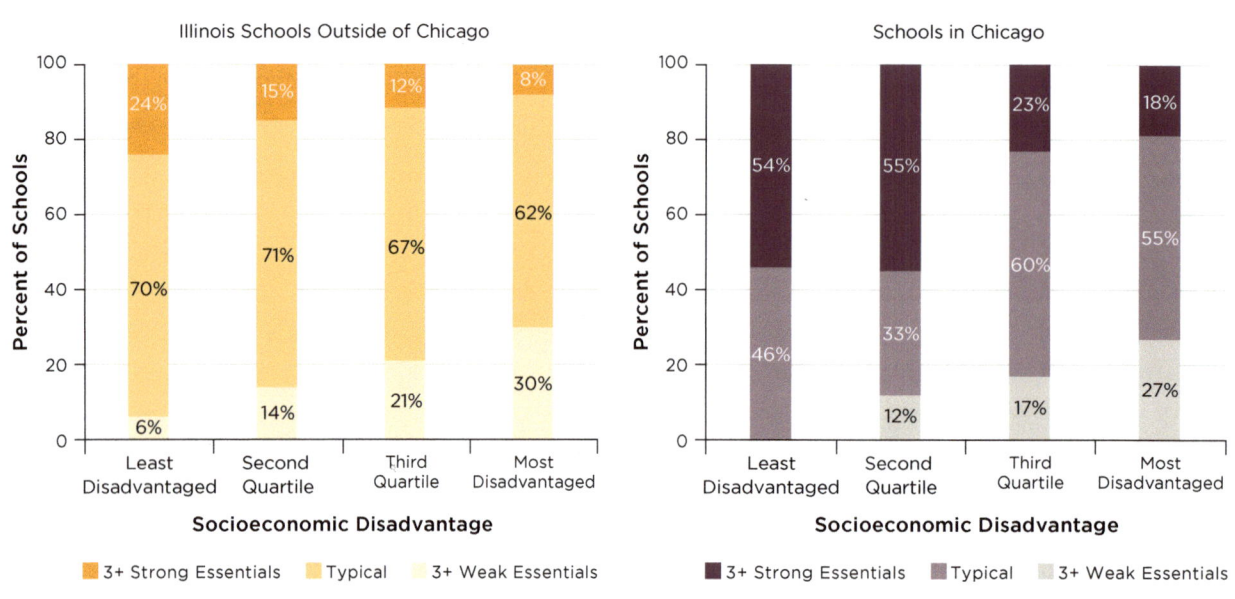

Strength in the Five Essentials by Socioeconomic Disadvantage

Note: The number in each of the columns represents the percentage of schools that fall into that category

---

[41] Muijs, Harris, Chapman, Stoll, & Russ (2004); Harris, Chapman, Muijs, Russ, & Stoll (2006).

CHAPTER 3

How the Essential Supports Relate to Student Outcomes

The essential supports framework suggests that a robust school organization fosters an environment conducive to learning. Prior research by UChicago CCSR suggests this is true in CPS. This study is a first look at whether or not essential supports are related with student outcomes in other settings.

We only have a single year of statewide survey data from the administration of the 5Essentials survey in 2013, and we only have student outcome data prior to and simultaneous with the survey. Therefore, it is too early to say one way or the other if strength in the essential supports actually causes better student outcomes in Illinois. Instead, we investigate if schools strong on the essential supports in 2013 had better student outcomes in data collected over the years of 2011–13. If schools strong on the essential supports had better outcomes in 2011–13, that would not prove the essential supports caused better outcomes. It could be that causality runs the other way, where better student outcomes resulted in stronger essentials. Alternatively, there may have been some unmeasured school factor that led them to have both better essential supports and better student outcomes. However, simply determining if there is a relationship between the essential supports and student outcomes in the multiple school contexts across Illinois is an important first step.

While in Chapter 2 we focused on the number of strong and weak essential supports a school has by community type, in this chapter we concentrate on schools' average essential supports (the average of schools' scores on effective leadership, collaborative teachers, involved families, supportive environment, and ambitious instruction), and the relationship of that average with student outcomes. We also examine how each individual essential support is related to outcomes, which are listed in the box titled **Student Outcomes in this Study**.

Student Outcomes in this Study

ISAT Math and Reading Test Score Levels: For both math and reading, we constructed a mean of a school's average scores in 2011, 2012, and 2013. By averaging over multiple years, we get a stable estimate for each school. This is referred to as *"levels"* to distinguish it from ISAT math and reading gains. Since only students in grades 3-8 take the ISAT test, this outcome is used only in analyses of elementary/middle schools.

ISAT Math and Reading Gains: For both math and reading scores, we calculated the average ISAT gain students experienced as they progressed from grade-to-grade in each school. This outcome is used only in analyses of elementary/middle schools.

Attendance Rate Level: The average of a school's attendance rates for 2011, 2012, and 2013.[R]

Attendance Rate Change: The average yearly change in a school's attendance rate for the 2011-2013 time period.

ACT Score Levels: At the time of data collection, all Illinois students took the ACT test in their junior year of high school. We constructed the mean of a school's average ACT scores for 2011, 2012, and 2013.

Graduation Rate Levels: The average of a high school's four-year graduation rates for 2011, 2012, and 2013.[S,T]

[R] ISBE calculates the attendance rate as the *"aggregate days of student attendance, divided by the sum of the aggregate days of student attendance and aggregate days of student absence."*

[S] ISBE calculates graduation rates by dividing the number of students in a cohort of first-time ninth-graders who earned a regular high school diploma within four years by the total number of students in that cohort (adding students who transferred into the school and substracting students who transferred out, emigrated, or died).

[T] Unfortunately, we could not calculate statistically reliable measures of change in graduation rates and ACT score. Graduation rates and average ACT scores fluctuated year-to-year, making it difficult to discern a linear time trend over three years. Random fluctuations were less of a problem with attendance rates.

Since CPS serves so many more students than any other district, we conducted our analyses separately for schools in CPS and schools in the rest of Illinois. K–5 schools were analyzed separately, because they had only three out of five essentials. **(See page 10 for an explanation of why K–5 schools are measured using only three essential supports.)**

Because schools strong on the essential supports may have other characteristics that contribute to having better student outcomes, such as an affluent student body **(see Chapter 2)**, we accounted for school differences in a variety of school and district characteristics. More information on our methods can be found in **Appendix A**.

Elementary School Findings

Strength in the essential supports is related to better student outcomes, particularly for ISAT learning gains.

Table 2 summarizes our results regarding the relationship between average essential supports and student outcomes, after accounting for differences that could be attributed to student body composition, urbanicity, charter status, and school size.

TABLE 2

Average Essential Supports Have Positive Associations with Elementary School Outcomes

Outcome	Illinois K–8, 6–8 Schools Outside CPS	CPS K–8, 6–8 Schools	Illinois K–5 Schools
ISAT Math Gains	+	+	+
ISAT Reading Gains	+	+	~
Attendance Rate Change	+	+	~
ISAT Math Average	+	+	+
ISAT Reading Average	+	+	+
Attendance Rate Average	+	~	+

Note: **+** The association between the average essential supports and the outcome is positive, statistically significant, and substantive.
+ The association between the average essential supports and the outcome is positive and statistically significant.
~ The association between the average essential supports and the outcome is not statistically significant.

When Is a Relationship Substantive?

When we did our analyses, we found that most of the time, strength in average essential supports was significantly related with superior student outcomes. *"Significantly"* means that we are confident the relationship exists in the population of Illinois schools, but that does not necessarily mean the relationship is a strong one. In education research there is no consensus for how strong an association has to be before we can conclude it is substantive.[U] To deal with this issue, we decided to use a benchmark related to school socioeconomic disadvantage to help us determine whether any relationship could be considered *"substantive."* We used socioeconomic disadvantage because it is one of the biggest determinants of student outcomes, and many policy interventions are motivated to reduce the gaps in performance between low-income and other students. When we present our results, we will note those associations that are statistically significant, but also those associations that are substantive, which we arbitrarily define as one-third of the size of the statewide association between the outcome and school socioeconomic disadvantage.[V] We note that our conclusions are very similar if we define a substantive association as one-half of the size of the association with school socioeconomic disadvantage. Interested readers who want to decide for themselves what a substantive association is are invited to consult **Appendix A Table A.6** which contains all of the standardized coefficients from these analyses.

U Lipsey et al. (2012).
V For example, the standardized coefficient for the association between socioeconomic disadvantage and high school graduation rates is -0.50 throughout Illinois (see Appendix Table A.6). The standardized coefficients for the association between the average essential supports and graduation rates is significant in high schools in CPS and in the rest of Illinois; the standardized coefficients are 0.12 outside of CPS and 0.30 in CPS. Because the coefficient for CPS is more than a third of 0.50, we say the relationship between schools' average essential support score and their graduation rate is substantive in CPS, but this relationship is not substantive in the rest of the state because 0.12 is less than a third of 0.50.

We use "+" signs to indicate associations that are positive, meaning that being strong on the average essential supports tends to go along with better outcomes. These associations are also statistically significant—we are confident an association truly exists and is not occurring due to random chance, but it does not necessarily mean an association is substantial. Out of the 18 associations we investigated for elementary schools, only three were not significant (and denoted with a tilde): the association with ISAT Reading Gains for K–5 schools, with attendance rate change for K–5 schools, and with attendance rates for CPS schools.[42] Plus ("+") signs that are in green are substantive associations. (See box *When Is a Relationship Substantive?*)

We illustrate the relationship between the essential supports and ISAT math gains in **Figure 7** (schools outside of CPS with K-8 and 6-8 grade configurations), **Figure 8** (CPS schools with K-8 and 6-8 grade configurations), and Figure 9 (K–5 schools inside and outside CPS). **Figure 7** includes annotations to help readers understand the charts presented in the remainder of this report. These figures show comparisons between schools weak on essential supports and schools strong on them, where *"weak"* means being at the 25th percentile and *"strong"* means being at the 75th percentile. These comparisons help us answer the question: what would the difference in student outcomes be if we compared two schools that had the same demographic characteristics but differed on their essential supports?

We also show a comparison between more socioeconomically disadvantaged schools (at the 75th percentile statewide) and less disadvantaged schools (at the 25th percentile statewide). The relationship between socioeconomic disadvantage and student outcomes allows readers to put the relationships involving essential supports in context. For more information on what the *"more disadvantaged"* and *"less disadvantaged"* schools look like, **see the box *What Do Schools at the 25th and 75th Percentile of Socioeconomic Disadvantage Look Like?***

What Do Schools at the 25th and 75th Percentile of Socioeconomic Disadvantage Look Like?

Figures 7 through 13 show the difference between schools at the 25th and 75th percentiles of socioeconomic disadvantage. To clarify what these schools look like, see Table A which includes information on the indicators used to calculate socioeconomic disadvantage. Schools at the 75th percentile of socioeconomic disadvantage have a far greater share of students eligible for free- and reduced-price lunches (70 percent versus 27 percent) and are located in census tracts with somewhat higher poverty rates (13 percent versus 4 percent) and male jobless rates (22 percent versus 13 percent).

TABLE A

Schools At the 75th Percentile of Socioeconomic Disadvantage Have Substantially Higher Shares of Impoverished Students Than Schools At the 25th Percentile

	Less Disadvantaged Schools (at 25th Percentile of Socioeconomic Disadvantage)	More Disadvantaged Schools (at the 75th Percentile of Socioeconomic Disadvantage)
Percent Eligible for Free or Reduced Lunch	27%	70%
Percent of Families At or Below the Poverty Line in the Surrounding Census Tract	4%	13%
Percent of Males Aged 16 or older who are jobless	13%	22%

---

[42] These associations were positive but small, with standardized regression coefficients of 0.03–0.04.

Overall, in Illinois K-8 and 6-8 schools outside CPS, the essential supports have a substantial positive association with ISAT math gains when compared to the effect of socioeconomic disadvantage. **Figure 7** shows the relationship between strength in the essential supports and student gains in ISAT math scores among schools outside CPS. Schools that have weak average essential supports have ISAT math gains of 10.3 ISAT points per year, while schools strong on the average essential supports gain 10.8 points per year (these numbers can also be found in **Appendix A Table A.7**). This is a difference of half of an ISAT point.

While this may seem relatively small, compare this to the relationship with socioeconomic disadvantage. Less disadvantaged schools have gains of about 11.3 ISAT points, while students at more disadvantaged schools have gains of 10.5 points, a difference of 0.8 ISAT points. This shows that in the rest of Illinois, the essential supports have an association with ISAT math gains that is more than half of the effect of being in the bottom versus top quartile in socioeconomic disadvantage.

For CPS, we see similar substantial relationships between the essential supports and students' ISAT math gains. **Figure 8** shows that students in CPS schools with strong essentials gain about 13.9 ISAT math points, while students in CPS schools with weak essentials gain 13.3 points—a difference of 0.6 ISAT points. The figure also contains what may be for some a surprising finding: ISAT math gains are on average greater in CPS schools than in those outside CPS. These findings are in line with research from the University of Illinois at Chicago showing that when one looks at test scores of groups of students defined by race and

How to Read Figures 7 Through 13

① Students in K-8 and 6-8 schools outside of CPS at the 25th percentile of essential supports gain 10.3 points on the ISAT math test per year, while students in schools at the 75th percentile gain 10.8 points per year. Going from weak to strong on the essential supports is associated with gaining an additional 0.5 points.

② We do the same analyses for each of the essential supports. Supportive environment has the biggest association while effective leaders has the weakest.

③ To put these effects in context, we show the effect of school socioeconomic disadvantage on ISAT math gains as well. Students in schools throughout Illinois at the 75th percentile of disadvantage gain 10.5 points on the ISAT math test, while students in schools at the 25th percentile (less disadvantaged) gain 11.3 points. Going from a disadvantaged school to a less disadvantaged school is associated with gaining an additional 0.8 points. The association with the essential supports (0.5) is about 60 percent of the association with socioeconomic disadvantage (0.8).

FIGURE 7

Strength in the Essential Supports Has Substantial Associations With Greater Student Math Gains in Illinois K-8 and 6-8 Schools Outside CPS

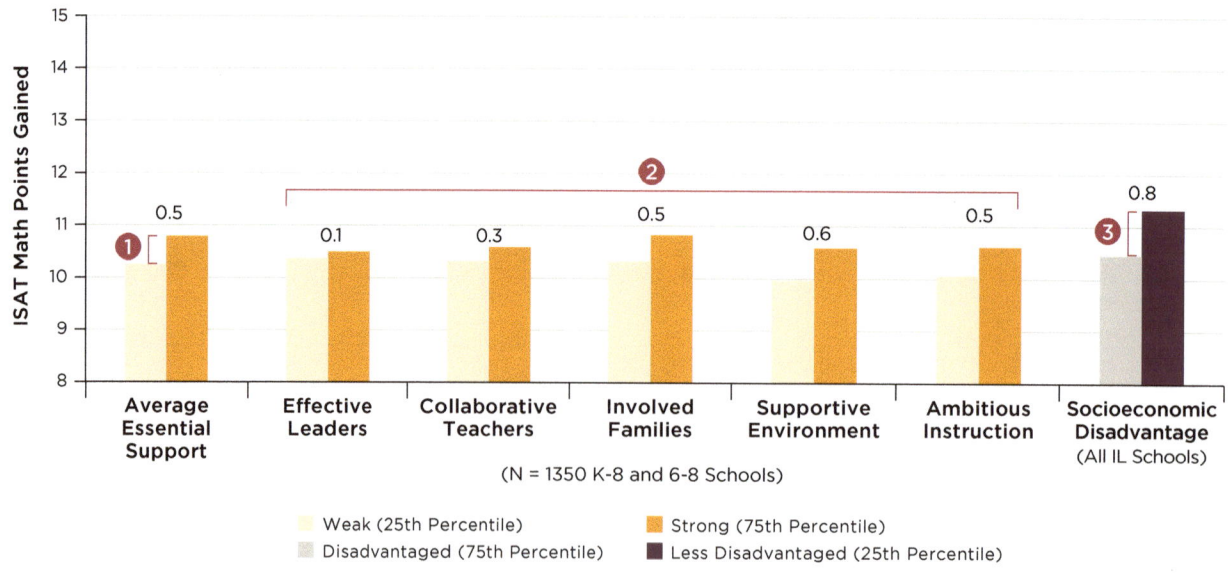

Note: School-level SD = 3.4 ISAT points. Numbers above bars represent the difference in the predicted outcome between the 25th percentile and the 75th percentile.

eligibility for free or reduced-price lunch, CPS students have recently started to outpace students in the rest of Illinois on the ISAT.[43,44]

The essential supports are associated with more ISAT learning gains in K–5 schools as well, but the associations are fairly small. Figure 9 shows that students in K–5 schools strong on the essential supports gain about 0.3 more points on the ISAT math test than students in K–5 schools with weak essential supports.[45]

Among elementary and middle schools, the essential supports as a whole are more strongly related with learning gains than they are with average scores or with attendance. As shown in **Table 2**, there are many positive associations between the essential supports and our other elementary school outcomes: ISAT mean *levels* (as opposed to gains), and attendance rate changes and levels. However, these associations are small.

There is a potential inconsistency here: the essential supports have relatively strong positive relationships with ISAT *gains* while having positive but weak associations with ISAT *levels*. ISAT levels reflect the cumulative influence of what students have learned in school and in the home while growing up, while ISAT gains reflect what the student has learned in the prior year, where the influence of school is arguably relatively greater. In other words, the essential supports have a smaller relationship with ISAT levels because it is harder for schools to overcome inequalities in accumulated learning grounded in disparities among both families and schools. However, it is easier for schools to overcome inequalities in what students learn from year-to-year.

FIGURE 8

Strength in the Essential Supports Has Substantial Associations With Greater Student Math Gains in CPS K-8 and 6-8 Schools

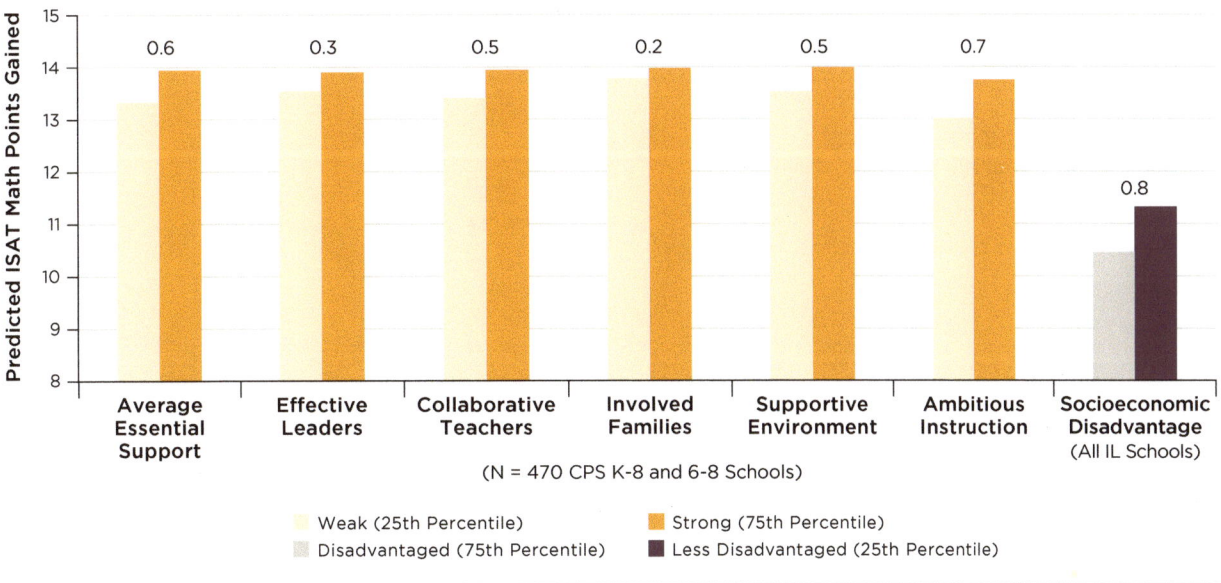

Note: School-level SD = 3.4 ISAT points. Numbers above bars represent the difference in the predicted outcome between the 25th percentile and the 75th percentile.

---

43 Zavitovsky (2015).
44 Readers may be struck by how low the bars are for the effect of socioeconomic disadvantage than they are for the bars for the effects of the essentials. While the gaps between the bars are comparable, the actual heights of the bars are not. The yellow bars are from a model examining only CPS schools with additional controls (school socioeconomic advantage and school racial composition), while the purple bars are from a model examining all Illinois schools.
45 The relationship is a third of the association between socioeconomic disadvantage and ISAT math gains, so it meets our definition of a *"substantive relationship;"* but the actual association is only significant at the 0.10 level, so we consider this an insubstantial relationship.

FIGURE 9

Strength in the Essential Supports Has Small Associations With Greater Student Math Gains in K-5 Schools in Illinois

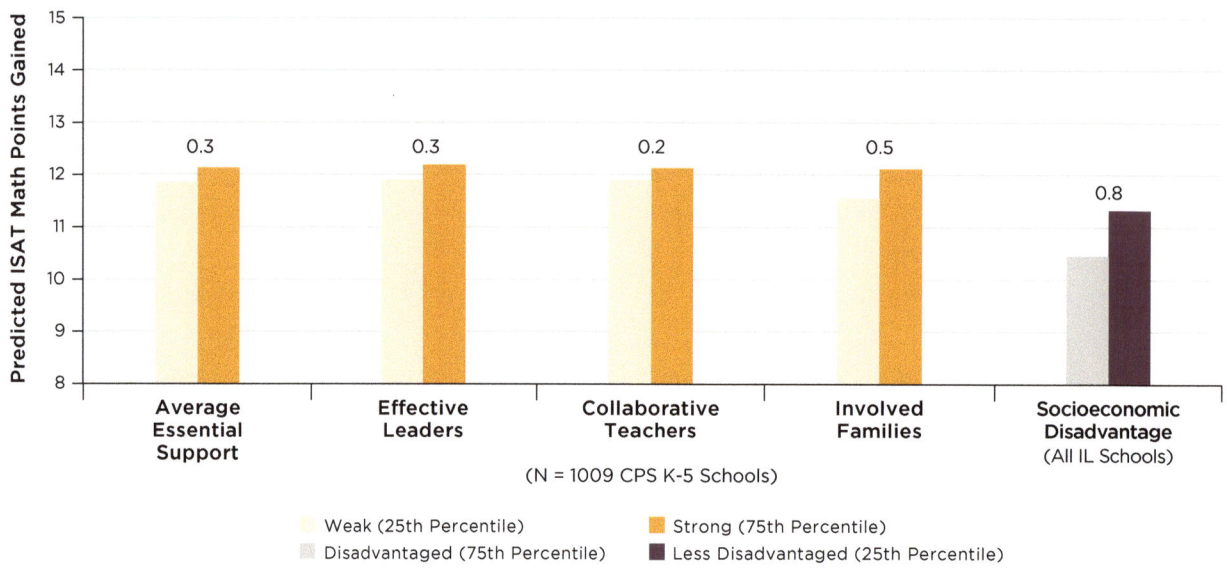

(N = 1009 CPS K-5 Schools)

- Weak (25th Percentile)
- Strong (75th Percentile)
- Disadvantaged (75th Percentile)
- Less Disadvantaged (25th Percentile)

Note: School-level SD = 3.4 ISAT points. Numbers above bars represent the difference in the predicted outcome between the 25th percentile and the 75th percentile.

High School Findings

Strength in the essential supports is related to better student outcomes, particularly in CPS schools

At the high school level, we analyze relationships between the essential supports and high school attendance rates, ACT scores, and four-year graduation rates—averaged over 2011–13—and the trend in attendance rates over the same period.

Table 3 shows that high schools strong on the essential supports have stronger outcomes throughout Illinois. These associations tend to be stronger in CPS schools (**see Appendix A Table A.6**).

Average ACT scores demonstrate this pattern. The relationship between the essential supports and ACT scores in the rest of Illinois is small. **Figure 10** shows that schools that have strong essential supports have average ACT scores of 19.6, which is only modestly greater than schools with weak supports, with average ACT scores of 19.3 (these numbers can be found in **Appendix A Table A.8**). This difference, 0.3 points, is much smaller than the difference between disadvantaged and less disadvantaged schools, which is 1.8 ACT points. When one examines the specific essential supports one at a time, supportive environment is the essential support with the largest relationship with ACT scores. Schools strong on supportive environment have higher ACT scores by 0.6 points than schools with weak supports, which approaches our definitions of *"substantive."*

In CPS schools (**shown in Figure 11**), strength on the essentials has a stronger association with higher ACT scores. Students in schools with strong essential supports score 1.1 points higher than students in schools with weak essential supports. As was the case

TABLE 3

Among High Schools, the Essential Supports Are Associated with Better Outcomes, Especially in CPS

Outcome	High Schools Outside CPS	CPS High Schools
Attendance Rate Change	+	+
Attendance Rate Average	+	+
ACT Average	+	+
4-Year Graduation Rate Average	+	+

+ The association between the average essential supports and the outcome is positive, statistically significant, and a greater than one-third of the size of the standardized coefficient for school socioeconomic disadvantage.
+ The association between the average essential supports and the outcome is positive, statistically significant, and less than a third of the size of the standardized coefficient for school socioeconomic disadvantage.

FIGURE 10

Strength in the Essential Supports Has Minimal Associations With Higher Average ACT Scores in High Schools Outside CPS

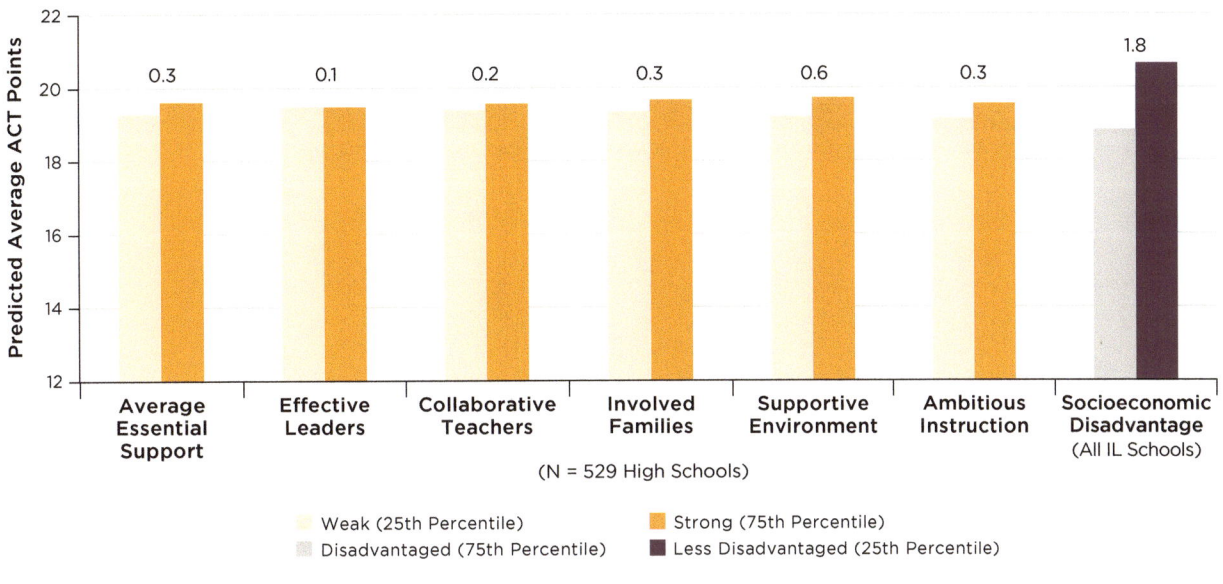

Note: School-level SD = 2.2 ACT points. Numbers above bars represent the difference in the predicted outcome between the 25th percentile and the 75th percentile.

FIGURE 11

Strength in the Essential Supports Has Substantial Associations With Higher Average ACT Scores in CPS

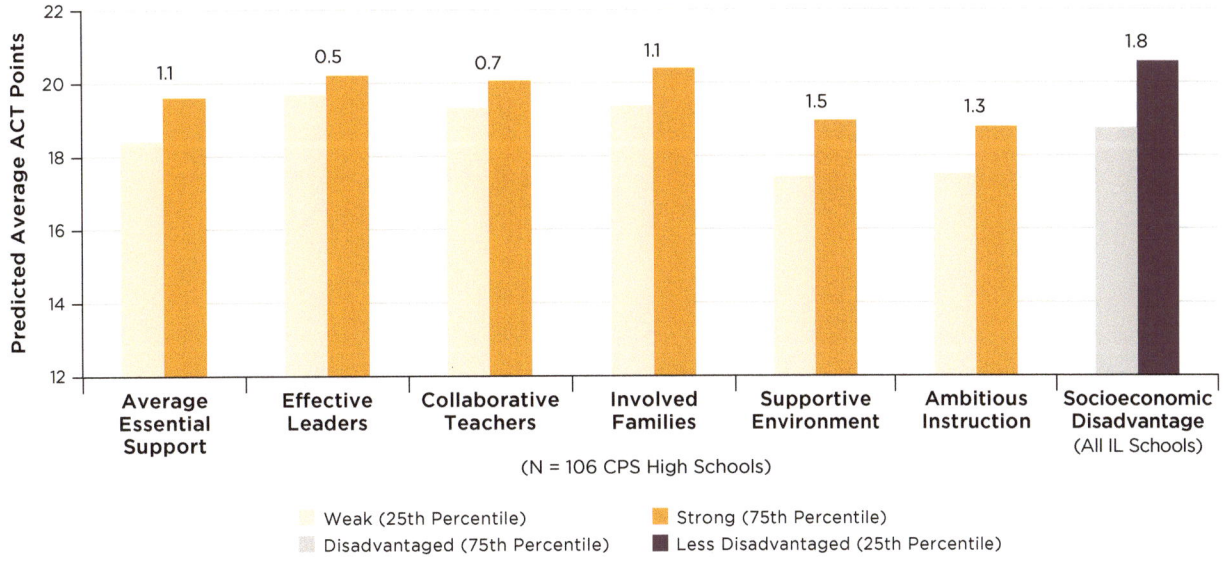

Note: School-level SD = 2.2 ACT points. Numbers above bars represent the difference in the predicted outcome between the 25th percentile and the 75th percentile.

with schools in the rest of Illinois, supportive environment has the strongest association with average ACT scores. The relatively large associations between supportive environment and high school outcomes has been documented in prior UChicago CCSR research on Chicago schools.[46]

Figures 12 and 13 show predicted graduation rates for high schools outside CPS and schools in CPS based on their essential supports; the results are very similar to those for ACT scores. In the rest of Illinois, schools

[46] Sebastian & Allensworth (2012).

with strong essential supports have higher graduation rates than schools with weak essential supports by 1.8 percentage points, but in CPS the difference is 5.2 percentage points. Outside of CPS, involved families and supportive environment are the essentials with the most substantial associations with graduation rates. Among Chicago high schools, all essentials have substantial associations with graduation rates.

FIGURE 12

Strength in the Essential Supports Has Modest Associations With Larger Graduation Rates in High Schools Outside CPS

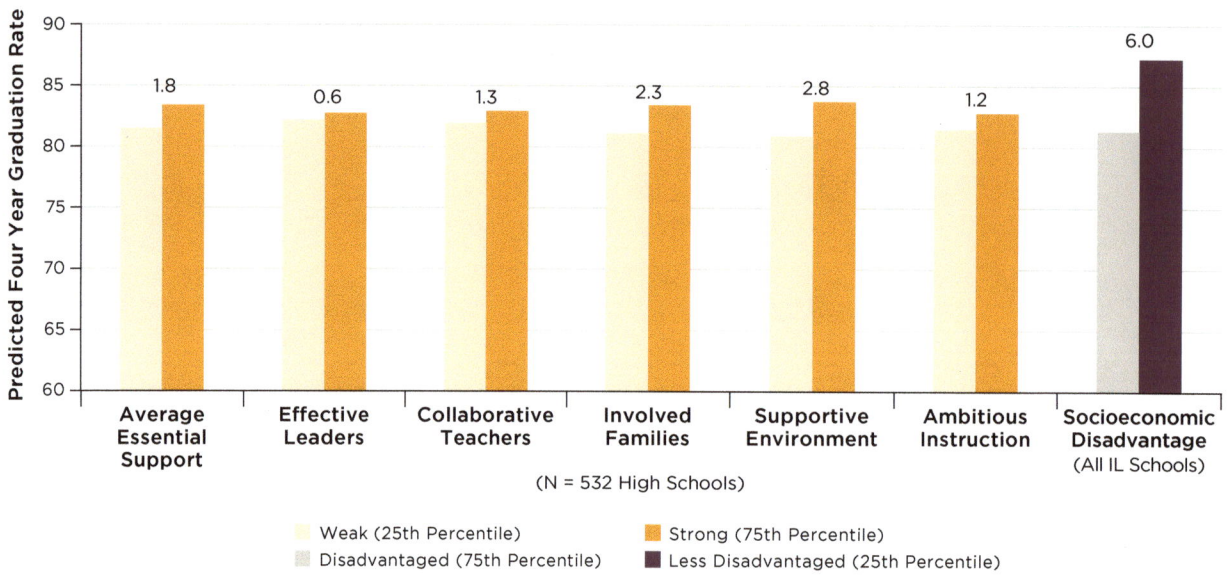

Note: School-level SD = 9.5 percentage points. Numbers above bars represent the difference in the predicted outcome between the 25th percentile and the 75th percentile.

FIGURE 13

Strength in the Essential Supports Has Substantial Associations With Larger Graduation Rates in CPS

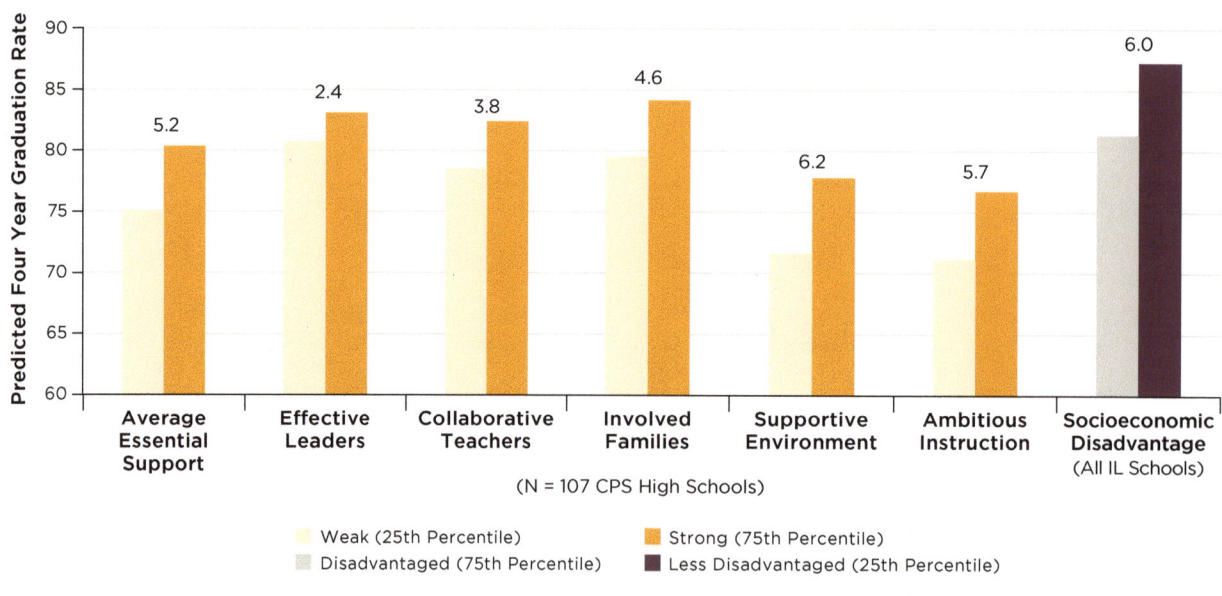

Note: School-level SD = 9.5 percentage points. Numbers above bars represent the difference in the predicted outcome between the 25th percentile and the 75th percentile.

CHAPTER 4

Interpretive Summary

At the heart of the essential supports framework is the idea that in order to improve student learning, schools must be organized to facilitate engaging and motivational instruction in classrooms. This entails schools with principals who are good managers and instructional leaders who meaningfully include teachers in decision-making; teachers who work together to improve instruction; demanding curricula that build on what students learned in prior grades; trust among school leaders, teachers, and parents; a safe, orderly, and supportive environment; and parents and community members who act as partners with the school in extending its mission.

This study, which examines nearly all public schools in Illinois, is a first look at how the essential supports framework operates across the whole state—in Chicago and smaller cities, suburbs, small towns, and rural areas. Because of data limitations, we cannot prove if the essential supports, as measured by the 5Essentials survey, actually influence student outcomes in Illinois. However, by examining if better student outcomes occur in schools with stronger essential supports in Illinois, we are taking a first step towards understanding what the essentials framework has to offer schools outside of Chicago.

Another goal of this study is to document disparities in essential supports across schools in the entire state. Regardless of whether or not the essential supports actually cause student learning, it is important to determine if communities and neighborhoods differ in their access to schools with strong essential supports. Most parents want their children to attend schools where principals are effective leaders; where teachers take collective responsibility for their students' learning and offer challenging instruction; where parents, teachers, and the principals trust each other; and where teachers and peers support students' academic pursuits.

Students in rural schools and socioeconomically disadvantaged schools are less likely to experience strong essential supports. The fact that students attending socioeconomically disadvantaged schools have much less access to the essential supports raises substantial equity concerns. Indeed, these students may be most in need of schools that are especially strong. Furthermore, students in rural and town schools have much less access to the essential supports than those in urban and suburban schools—especially in high schools—which is also concerning. It is important to note that locational inequalities are strongest in ambitious instruction, the essential that is theorized to have the most direct influence on student outcomes.

Our findings revealed that the largest percentage of schools strong in climate and instruction in Illinois are located in urban and suburban communities. It is important to acknowledge that schools located in more urbanized areas may have access to particular benefits that rural schools do not have. CPS schools, for example, have the benefit of a large, centralized school district that can take advantage of economies of scale. Chicago itself is the home of many institutional resources (diverse vendors, nonprofit organizations, universities, and foundations) that probably play no small role in fostering the essential supports. Schools outside of Chicago, especially rural schools, have much less access to these kinds of resources. These resources do not guarantee strong essentials—CPS schools are the lowest on family involvement, and non-rural schools outside CPS rank higher on supportive environment—yet CPS schools are the most likely to have effective leaders, collaborative teachers, and ambitious instruction.

For policymakers, these findings suggest that it is important to identify the obstacles confronting schools in developing strong essential supports, and what can be done to assist schools in strengthening their practices.

For local stakeholders, paying attention to their 5Essentials school reports (the 2014 results are available at https://illinois.5-essentials.org/2014_public/) could be useful in addressing these disparities. These reports contain information on teachers' and students' ratings of the various essential supports. By studying their school survey reports, school and district staff, parents, and interested citizens can see how students and teachers perceive their schools, including the ways in which they are doing well, and the areas where concerns are indicated. These reports are not a magic bullet guaranteeing school improvement. Rather, the goal is for them to serve as springboards for conversations between school leaders, teachers, and parents over what is working and what is not in schools, and how these groups can collaborate to strengthen the school organization.

Early evidence indicates strength in the essential supports is positively related to important student outcomes, although the size of the association varies by school context. Our findings indicate that student learning is better in schools with stronger essential supports. This association is particularly strong for important student outcomes like ISAT test score growth (both math and reading) across the state, and average ACT scores and graduation rates in Chicago high schools.

However, for other outcomes the associations tend to be rather weak. This is the case for high schools outside of Chicago. The essential supports also have weak associations with ISAT levels, attendance rates, and improvement in attendance rates in elementary schools.

Some of this is to be expected. As noted before, ISAT levels reflect the influences of family background to a greater extent than test score gains, and it is not surprising that the essentials have a small relationship with test score levels.

In some instances, we can only offer speculative accounts to explain small associations. The essential supports have inconsistent effects on ISAT gains in K-5 schools. One possibility is that this could be due to the lack of data on all of the essential supports in K-5 schools. Students in grades below six were not surveyed, and thus we are missing information on K-5 schools' levels of supportive environment and ambitious instruction. These two essential supports had some of the larger associations with ISAT gains in Illinois schools. If we had information on them in K–5 schools the average of the five essentials (rather than the *"three essentials"*) may have had stronger associations.

There is no immediate explanation for why the essential supports have substantial associations in CPS high schools, but not in high schools in the rest of the state. One possibility is that the survey questions resonate less with high school teachers and students outside of Chicago, suggesting the need to explore new survey questions that better gauge the experiences of those populations.

The insubstantial (and sometimes nonexistent) direct associations we found between effective leadership and student outcomes is noteworthy. However, it is in line with prior research showing that the relationship between leadership and student learning appears to be indirect.[47] These studies posit that leadership works through other organizational mechanisms such as teacher professional community and school climate/culture to influence learning.[48] Recent research in CPS schools also showed that school leaders have a small and indirect relationship with student achievement growth.[49] Our findings, on the other hand, showed a weak association between leadership and student outcomes, which could indicate that the survey measures used to capture this concept are missing important aspects of what effec-

---

[47] Leithwood et al. (2004) in their review of the literature, claim that the total relationship (both direct and indirect) can account for up to a quarter of the total school effects on student learning. (See Hallinger & Heck, 1996; Leithwood & Jantzi, 2000). Sebastian & Allensworth (2012), for example, found that high school leadership was associated with student achievement primarily via the school climate. Bryk and his colleagues (2010) undertook a longitudinal analysis that revealed that the base level of leadership was associated with subsequent changes in strength of the other four essentials supports (Bryk et al., 2010, Chapter 4).

[48] See Louis et al. (2010) for example.

[49] Sebastian, Allensworth & Huang (forthcoming).

tive school leaders do. As the state of Illinois continues to deploy the 5Essentials survey throughout its schools, future research should consider this explanation.

Future research will examine why the relationships are stronger for some outcomes and contexts than in others. The 5Essentials survey is a living and breathing instrument that is tweaked year-to-year based on the efficacy of measurement and ongoing research questions. This report's findings point to future directions for the survey. The weak relationships between essential supports and ISAT gains for K–5 schools underscore the need for student surveys in K–5 schools, and UChicago CCSR is piloting surveys for students in the fourth and fifth grades. Another finding is the relatively weak relationships between the five essential supports and student outcomes for high schools outside of CPS, indicating there may be better ways to capture the essential supports in those contexts. Finally, and most importantly, by collecting and accumulating data for Illinois schools in the future, researchers will be able to rigorously study whether or not the essential supports actually influence school improvement in all of Illinois.

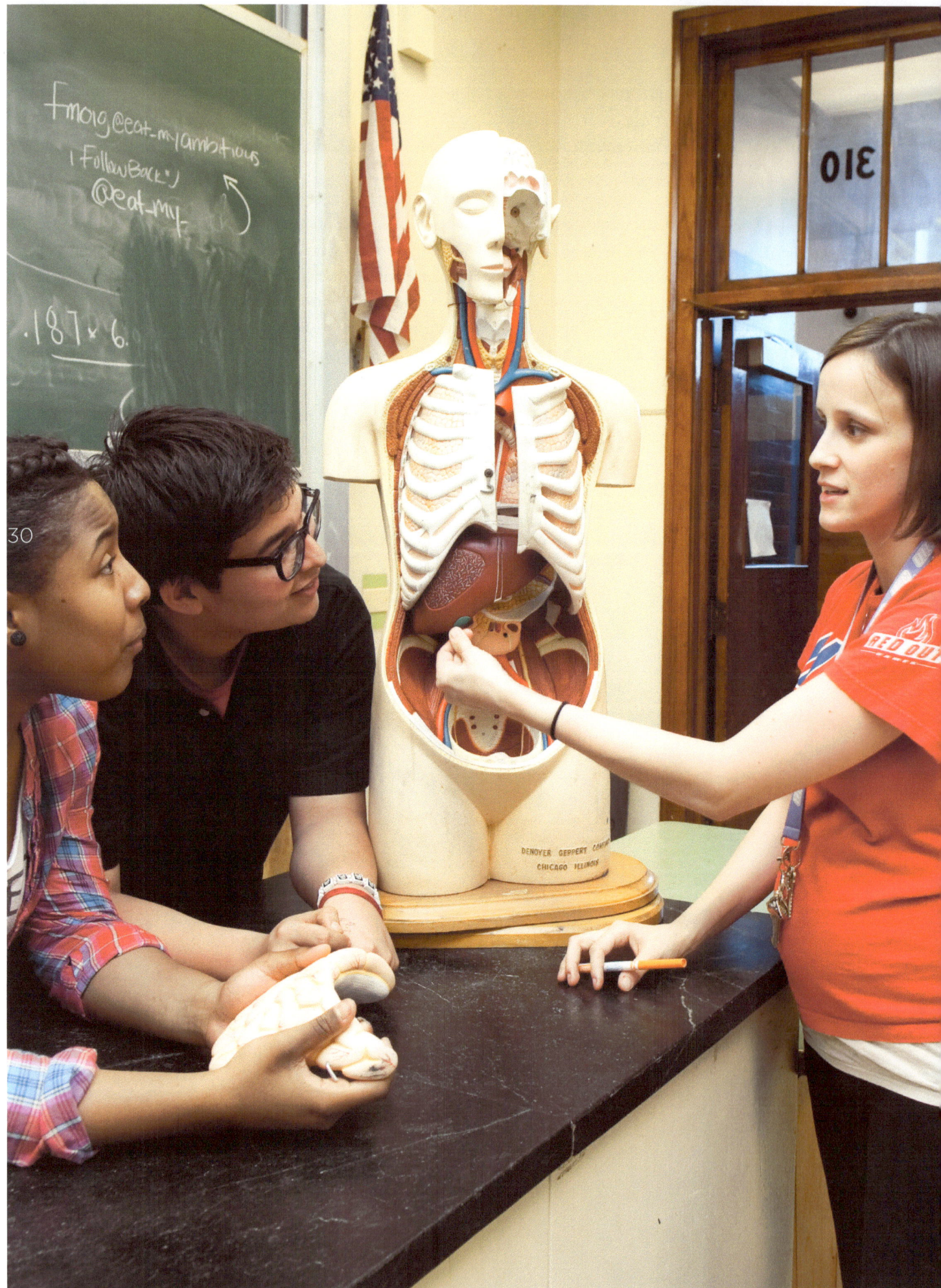

References

Bowen, N.K., & Bowen, G.L. (1999). Effects of crime and violence in neighborhoods and schools on the school behavior and performance of adolescents. *Journal of Adolescent Research, 14*(3), 319–342.

Bryk, A.S., Sebring, P.B., Allensworth, E., Luppescu, S., & Easton, J.Q. (2010). *Organizing school improvement: Lessons from Chicago.* Chicago, IL: University of Chicago Press.

Byun, S.Y., Meece, J.L., & Irvin, M.J. (2012). Rural-nonrural disparities in postsecondary educational attainment revisited. *American Educational Research Journal, 49*(3), 412–437.

Crosnoe, R., Johnson, M.K., & Elder, G.H. (2004). School size and the interpersonal side of education: An examination of race/ethnicity and organizational context. *Social Science Quarterly, 85*(5), 1259–1274.

Forsyth, P.B., Barnes, L.L., & Adams, C.M. (2006). Trust-effectiveness patterns in schools. *Journal of Educational Administration, 44*(2), 122–141.

Ginsburg-Block, M.D., & Fantuzzo, J.W. (1998). An evaluation of the relative effectiveness of NCTM standards-based interventions for low-achieving urban elementary students. *Journal of Educational Psychology, 90*(3), 560–569.

Goddard, R.D., Sweetland, S.R., & Hoy, W.K. (2000). Academic emphasis of urban elementary schools and student achievement in reading and mathematics: A multilevel analysis. *Educational Administration Quarterly, 36*(5), 683–702.

Goddard, Y.L., Goddard, R.D., & Tschannen-Moran, M. (2007). A theoretical and empirical investigation of teacher collaboration for school improvement and student achievement in public elementary schools. *Teachers College Record, 109*(4), 877–896.

Goddard, R.D., Tschannen-Moran, M., & Hoy, W.K. (2001). A multilevel examination of the distribution and effects of teacher trust in students and parents in urban elementary schools. *The Elementary School Journal, 102*(1), 3–17.

Grissom, J.A., & Loeb, S. (2011). Triangulated principal effectiveness: How perspectives of parents, teachers, and assistant principals identify the central importance of managerial skills. *American Educational Research Journal, 48*(3), 1091–1123.

Grissom, J.A., Loeb, S., & Master, B. (2013). Effective instructional time use for school leaders: Longitudinal evidence from observations of principals. *Educational Researcher, 42*(8), 433–444.

Grossman, P., Loeb, S., Cohen, J., Hammerness, K., Wyckoff, J., Boyd, D., & Lankford, H. (2010). *Measure for measure: The relationship between measures of instructional practice in middle school English language arts and teachers' value-added scores (*NBER Working Paper No. w16015). Cambridge, MA: National Bureau of Economic Research. Retrieved from http://www.nber.org/papers/w16015

Hallinger, P., & Heck, R.H. (1996). Reassessing the principal's role in school effectiveness: A review of empirical research, 1980–95. *Educational Administration Quarterly, 32*(1), 5–44.

Hallinger, P., & Heck, R.H. (1998). Exploring the principal's contribution to school effectiveness: 1980–1995. *School Effectiveness and School Improvement: An International Journal of Research, Policy, and Practice, 9*(2), 157–191.

Hallinger, P., & Heck, R.H. (2010). Leadership for learning: Does collaborative leadership make a difference in school improvement? *Educational Management Administration & Leadership, 38*(6), 654–678.

Hardré, P.L., Sullivan, D.W., & Crowson, H.M. (2009). Student characteristics and motivation in rural high schools. *Journal of Research in Rural Education, 24*(16), 1–19.

Hargreaves, A., & Fullan, M. (2012). *Professional capital: Transforming teaching in every school.* New York, NY: Teachers College Press.

Harris, A., Chapman, C., Muijs, D., Russ, J., & Stoll, L. (2006). Improving schools in challenging contexts: Exploring the possible. *School Effectiveness and School Improvement, 17*(4), 409–424.

Hoy, W.K., Tarter, C.J., & Hoy, A.W. (2006). Academic optimism of schools: A force for student achievement. *American Educational Research Journal, 43*(3), 425–446.

Illinois State Board of Education. (n.d.a). Learning Conditions Survey. Retrieved from http://www.isbe.net/peac/pdf/learning_cond_survey.pdf.

Illinois State Board of Education. (n.d.b). Illinois report card 2013-2014. Retrieved from http://illinoisreportcard.com/

Illinois State Board of Education News. (2013, January 30). School Environment Matters: State Board of Education administers first Illinois 5Essentials Survey to help improve student learning. Students, parents and teachers weigh in on school climate and learning conditions. Retrieved from http://www.isbe.state.il.us/news/2013/jan30.htm

Jeynes, W. (2003). A meta-analysis of parental involvement on minority children's academic achievement. *Education and Urban Society, 35*(2), 202-218.

Jeynes, W. (2007). The relationship between parental involvement and urban secondary school student academic achievement: A meta-analysis. *Urban Education, 42*(1), 82-110.

Jeynes, W. (2012). A meta-analysis of the efficacy of different types of parental involvement programs for urban students. *Urban Education, 47*(4), 706-742.

Johnson, S.M., Kraft, M.A., & Papay, J.P. (2012). How context matters in high-need schools: The effects of teachers' working conditions on their professional satisfaction and their students' achievement. *Teachers College Record, 114*(10), 1-39.

Klem, A.M., & Connell, J.P. (2004). Relationships matter: Linking teacher support to student engagement and achievement. *Journal of School Health, 74*(7), 262–273.

Leithwood, K., & Jantzi, D. (2009). A review of empirical evidence about school size effects: A policy perspective. *Review of Educational Research, 79*(1), 464–490.

Leithwood, K., & Jantzi, D. (2000). The effects of transformational leadership on organizational conditions and student engagement with school. *Journal of Educational Administration, 38*(2), 112-129.

Leithwood, K., Louis, K., Anderson, S., & Wahlstrom, K. (2004). *Review of research: How leadership influences student learning.* Ontario, Canada: Center for Applied Research and Educational Improvement, Ontario Institute for Studies in Education

Leithwood, K., & Louis, K.S. (2012). *Linking leadership to student learning.* San Francisco, CA: John Wiley & Sons.

Lipsey, M.W., Puzio, K., Yun, C., Hebert, M.A., Steinka-Fry, K., Cole, M.W., Roberts, M., Anthony, K.S., & Busick, M.D. (2012). *Translating the statistical representation of the effects of education interventions into more readily interpretable forms* (NCSER 2013-3000). Washington, DC: National Center for Special Education Reseach, U.S. Department of Education.

Louis, K.S., Leithwood, K.L., Wahlstrom, K., Anderson, S.E., Michlin, M., Mascall, B., Gordon, M.F., Strauss, T., Thomas, E., & Moore, S. (2010). *Learning from leadership: Investigating the links to improved student learning.* Final report of research to the Wallace Foundation. Minneapolis, MN: University of Minnesota.

Matsumura, L.C., Slater, S.C., & Crosson, A. (2008). Classroom climate, rigorous instruction and curriculum, and students' interactions in urban middle schools. *Elementary School Journal, 108*(4): 293–312.

Muijs, D., Harris, A., Chapman, C., Stoll, L., & Russ, J. (2004). Improving schools in socioeconomically disadvantaged areas: A review of research evidence. *School Effectiveness and School Improvement, 15*(2), 149–175.

Reys, R., Reys, B., Lapan, R., Holliday, G., & Wasman, D. (2003). Assessing the impact of "standards"-based middle grades mathematics curriculum materials on student achievement. *Journal for Research in Mathematics Education, 34*(1), 74–95.

Robinson, V.M., Lloyd, C.A., & Rowe, K.J. (2008). The impact of leadership on student outcomes: An analysis of the differential effects of leadership types. *Educational Administration Quarterly, 44*(5), 635–674.

Robers, S., Kemp, J., & Truman, J. (2013). *Indicators of school crime and safety: 2012.* (NCES 2013-036/NCJ 241446). Washington, DC: National Center for Education Statistics. Retrieved from http://nces.ed.gov/pubs2013/2013036.pdf

Roscigno, V.J., Tomaskovic-Devey, D., & Crowley, M. (2006). Education and the inequalities of place. *Social Forces, 84*(4), 2121–2145.

Sebastian, J., & Allensworth, E. (2012). The influence of principal leadership on classroom instruction and student learning: A study of mediated pathways to learning. *Educational Administration Quarterly, 48*(4), 626–663.

Sebastian, J., & Allensworth, E. (2012). How do secondary principals influence teaching and learning? *Principal's Research Review, 8*(4), 1–5.

Sebastian, J., Allensworth, E., & Huang, H. (forthcoming). *Principal and Teacher Leadership in Schools: A Mediational Analysis.* Unpublished manuscript.

Sheldon, S.B., & Epstein, J.L. (2005). Involvement counts: Family and community partnerships and mathematics achievements. *Journal of Education Research, 98*(4), 196–207.

Stronge, J.H., Ward, T.J., Tucker, P.D., & Hindman, J.L. (2007). What is the relationship between teacher quality and student achievement? An exploratory study. *Journal of Personnel Evaluation in Education, 20*(3), 165–184.

UChicago Impact: Tools for reliably excellent schooling. (2011, July 1).
Retrieved from uchicagoimpact.org

Wahlstrom, K.L., & Louis, K.S. (2008).
How teachers experience principal leadership: The roles of professional community, trust, efficacy, and shared responsibility. *Educational Administration Quarterly, 44*(4), 458–495.

Wenglinsky, H. (2000).
How teaching matters: Bringing the classroom back into discussions of teacher quality. Princeton, NJ: Educational Testing Service.

Witziers, B., Bosker, R.J., & Krüger, M.L. (2003).
Educational leadership and student achievement: The elusive search for an association. *Educational Administration Quarterly, 39*(3), 398–425.

Zavitovsky, P. (2015).
The changing face of achievement in Chicago and the rest of Illinois. Chicago, IL: University of Illinois-Chicago, Center for Urban Education Leadership.

Appendix A
Data and Methods

Description of Illinois Schools

TABLE A.1
Number and Percent of Schools in Illinois by Location

Location	Elem./Middle Schools	High Schools	Total Number	Total Percent
CPS	478	111	589	16.0
Urban Non-CPS	337	38	375	10.2
Suburban	1221	150	1371	37.2
Town	349	116	465	12.6
Rural	653	231	884	24.0
Total	**3,038**	**646**	**3,684**	**100.0**

Note: This table represents only schools with valid 5Essentials data (85 percent of Illinois schools).

TABLE A.3
Number and Percent of Illinois Schools by Enrollment (School Size)

Student Enrollment	Elem./Middle Schools	High Schools	Total Number	Total Percent
1–199	372	125	497	14.0
200–299	487	75	562	15.4
300–399	603	61	664	18.3
400–499	558	42	600	16.1
500–599	384	35	419	11.1
600–699	242	27	269	7.2
700–999	300	49	349	9.3
1,000+	92	232	324	8.6
Total	**3,038**	**646**	**3,684**	**100.0**

Note: This table represents only schools with valid 5Essentials data (85 percent of Illinois schools).

TABLE A.2
Correlations Among the Essential Supports

	Collaborative Teachers	Involved Families	Supportive Environment	Ambitious Instruction
Effective Leaders	0.76	0.54	0.31	0.34
Collaborative Teachers		0.72	0.50	0.47
Involved Families			0.56	0.39
Supportive Environment				0.74

TABLE A.4
Socioeconomic Disadvantage within Location: Percent and Number of Illinois Elementary/Middle Schools and High Schools

Location	Least Disadvantaged	Second Quartile	Third Quartile	Most Disadvantaged
CPS	3.9 (23)	6.3 (37)	10.2 (60)	79.6 (469)
Urban Non-CPS	27.7 (104)	17.9 (67)	24.8 (93)	29.6 (111)
Suburban	37.4 (513)	21.7 (298)	23.3 (319)	17.6 (241)
Town	11.4 (53)	31.2 (145)	42.8 (199)	14.6 (68)
Rural	25.2 (223)	42.3 (374)	27.7 (245)	4.8 (42)

Note: This table represents only schools with valid 5Essentials data (85 percent of Illinois schools).

Data and Methods

5Essentials Surveys of Teachers and Students

The Illinois State Board of Education contracted with UChicago Impact to administer the survey to Illinois teachers and students in the spring of 2013 (from February 1st to April 12th), for the purpose of providing data back to schools on the essential supports framework. Students in grades 6-12 and all full-time classroom teachers in public schools in Illinois were eligible to take the survey. Out of 152,462 teachers in Illinois, 104,270 (68 percent) took the survey, and out of 1,101,025 students in grades 6-12 in Illinois, 750,329 (68 percent) completed the survey. Survey data were collected via web. School staff facilitated data collection among students and monitored response rates for both students and teachers.

For details on how the 5Essential data were scored, please see **http://help.5-essentials.org/customer/portal/articles/94413-how-scores-are-calculated**. While the 2013 results are not publicly available, for 2014, the complete 5Essentials report for each participating school is available at **https://illinois.5essentials.org/2014_public/**.

The Essential Supports

Because the essential supports framework was being tested outside of Chicago for the first time in 2013, we analyzed how reliable the survey measures (which make up the essential supports) were across different school contexts. *"Reliability"* captures how well we can distinguish a measure across different schools. This is based on the number of respondents in the school and

TABLE A.5
Reliabilities of All Survey Measures Used to Construct the Essential Supports

Essential	Measure	Respondent	Outside CPS				CPS	
			ES	HS	K-5	6-8	ES	HS
Ambitious Instruction	Course Clarity	Student	0.69	0.73	—	0.82	0.82	0.86
Ambitious Instruction	English Instruction	Student	0.78	0.85	—	0.88	0.86	0.92
Ambitious Instruction	Math Instruction	Student	0.79	0.81	—	0.89	0.85	0.92
Ambitious Instruction	Quality of Student Discussion	Teacher	0.57	0.60	—	0.67	0.71	0.76
Collaborative Teachers	Collective Responsibility	Teacher	0.77	0.74	0.74	0.78	0.79	0.84
Collaborative Teachers	Quality Professional Development	Teacher	0.73	0.71	0.72	0.74	0.74	0.73
Collaborative Teachers	School Commitment	Teacher	0.77	0.80	0.77	0.82	0.83	0.84
Collaborative Teachers	Teacher-Teacher Trust	Teacher	0.76	0.73	0.77	0.80	0.76	0.78
Effective Leaders	Principal Instructional Leadership	Teacher	0.84	0.84	0.85	0.85	0.83	0.81
Effective Leaders	Program Coherence	Teacher	0.83	0.81	0.82	0.83	0.79	0.81
Effective Leaders	Teacher Influence	Teacher	0.84	0.80	0.83	0.85	0.85	0.82
Effective Leaders	Teacher-Principal Trust	Teacher	0.83	0.85	0.86	0.86	0.83	0.83
Involved Families	Community Resources	Student	0.88	0.93	—	0.96	0.93	0.94
Involved Families	Outreach to Parents	Teacher	0.73	0.75	0.76	0.78	0.78	0.77
Involved Families	Teacher-Parent Trust	Teacher	0.80	0.80	0.83	0.84	0.82	0.86
Supportive Environment	Academic Personalism	Student	0.72	0.71	—	0.83	0.86	0.87
Supportive Environment	Academic Press	Student	0.67	0.75	—	0.85	0.86	0.92
Supportive Environment	Peer Support for Academic Work	Student	0.74	0.82	—	0.89	0.85	—
Supportive Environment	Postsecondary Expectations	Teacher	—	0.89	—	—	—	0.92
Supportive Environment	Safety	Student	0.82	0.90	—	0.94	0.93	0.97
Supportive Environment	School-Wide Future Orientations	Student	—	0.86	—	—	—	0.93
Supportive Environment	Student-Teacher Trust	Student	0.84	0.85	—	0.92	0.91	0.93

Appendix A

how consistently respondents answer the survey questions within a school. For example, if we try to estimate the measure *"collective responsibility"* (which is based on teacher responses), reliability will be low if we have low numbers of teachers within all schools answering the *"collective responsibility"* items, or if teachers within schools answer the *"collective responsibility"* items in different ways (some reporting low collective responsibility and others reporting high collective responsibility). **Table A.5** presents the reliabilities for all of the measures used in this study for schools in Chicago and schools in the rest of the state. Most of the reliabilities in and out of Chicago are above 0.70.

Outcome Indicators

Our outcomes (ISAT scores, attendance rates, ACT scores, and four-year graduation rates) are taken from official ISBE data collected in the springs of 2011, 2012, and 2013.

ISAT Learning Gains

Our data on ISAT scores has a three-level structure: student observations are nested within students, which in turn are nested in schools. We estimated an effect of time ($\varpi 1$) specific to students and schools, which represents learning gains. To account for the fact that students' learning gains tend to taper off at the higher grades, we controlled for students' initial grade when they entered the data. To also make sure our outcomes are not affected by changing demographics in the school, we controlled for a student's receipt of free or reduced-price lunch and their homeless and Limited-English-Proficiency status, as well as race. For each school, we extracted Empirical Bayes estimates of β_{10k}, the average learning gains, as well as β_{00k}, the average initial test scores (in 2011). Average initial test scores served as a control variable when we examined learning gains.

Our multilevel models are presented below. i indexes student-observations, j indexes students, and k indexes schools.

$$Y_{ijk} = \pi_{0jk} + \pi_{1jk}(YEAR_{ijk} - 2011) + \pi_2(freelunch_{ijk}) + \pi_3(homeless_{ijk}) + \pi_4(LEP)_{ijk} + e_{ijk}$$

$$\pi_{0jk} = \beta_{00k} + \beta_{01}(initial\ grade_{jk}) + \beta_{02}(Asian_{jk}) + \beta_{03}(Black_{jk}) + \beta_{04}(Hispanic_{jk}) + \beta_{05}(Otherrace_{jk}) + r_{0jk}$$

$$\pi_{1jk} = \beta_{10k} + \beta_{11}(initial\ grade_{jk}) + r_{1jk}$$

$$\beta_{00k} = \gamma_{00} + u_{00k}$$

$$\beta_{10k} = \gamma_{10} + u_{10k}$$

- **Freelunch** is an indicator for whether or not the student received a free or reduced-price lunch.
- **Homeless** is an indicator for whether or not the student (or his/her parents) have reported to the school that s/he is homeless.
- **LEP** is an indicator for whether or not the student has Limited English Proficiency.
- **Initial Grade** is the grade level of a student when s/he is first observed in the data covering the 2010-11, 2011-12, and 2012-13 school years.
- **Asian, Black, Hispanic, and Otherrace** are indicators for student race.

ISAT Score Levels

We also used a three-level multilevel model to estimate schools' average test score over the 2011–13 time period, although we only controlled for students' initial grade. Empirical Bayes estimates of β_{00k}, schools' average test scores, were extracted and used as outcomes. As above, i indexes student-observations, j indexes students, and k indexes schools.

$$Y_{ijk} = \pi_{0jk} + e_{ijk}$$

$$\pi_{0jk} = \beta_{00k} + \beta_{01}(initial\ grade_{jk}) + r_{0jk}$$

$$\beta_{00k} = \gamma_{000} + u_{00k}$$

Attendance Rate Change

To see if schools are improving on any school-level outcomes, for each school we estimated a time trend in attendance rates. We again used a multilevel model to do this. In order to remove any effects of changes in schools' observed demographics, we controlled for the percent of students who received free or reduced-price lunch, who were homeless, who were of Limited English Proficiency status, who were black, and who were Hispanic.

Our multilevel models are below. j indexes school-observations and k indexes schools.

$$Y_{jk} = \beta_{0k} + \beta_{1k}(\text{year}_{jk} - 2011) + \beta_2(\%\text{freelunch}_{jk}) + \beta_3(\%\text{homeless}_{jk}) + \beta_4(\%\text{LEP}_{jk}) + \beta_5(\%\text{Black}_{jk}) + \beta_6(\%\text{Hispanic}_{jk}) + r_{jk}$$

$$\beta_{0k} = \gamma_{00} + u_{0k}$$

$$\beta_{1k} = \gamma_{10} + u_{1k}$$

- **Percent Freelunch** is the percent of students receiving a free or reduced-price lunch.
- **Percent Homeless** is the percent of students whose families have notified schools they are homeless.
- **Percent LEP** is the percent of students who have Limited English Proficiency status.
- **Percent Black** and **Percent Hispanic** are the percentages of students in the school who are Black and Hispanic, respectively.

We generated estimates of β_{1k}, each school's time trend, and β_{0k}, each school's initial value of the outcome in 2011.[50]

Attendance Rate, ACT Score, and Graduation Rate Levels

From ISBE, we have data on outcomes reported at the school level for 2011, 2012, and 2013: ACT composite scores, attendance rates, and four-year graduation rates. We averaged all three years of data for these outcomes for each school.

Analyzing the Association Between the Essential Supports and Student Outcomes

We estimated school-level linear regressions to analyze associations between the essential supports and student outcomes. We ran our models separately for CPS schools (excluding K-5 schools), schools outside of CPS (excluding K-5 schools), and K-5 schools. For K-8, 6-8, and K-5 schools, we used district fixed effects models to account for any potential district-level factors that could affect both schools' level of essential supports and student outcomes. We could not do this for high schools because 75 percent of high schools were the only high school in their district in our data, so we controlled for a number of district-level characteristics instead.

Our basic model for high schools is presented below. The models for K-8, 6-8, and K5 schools are similar, but since we used district fixed effects models the district-level controls are omitted. k indexes schools:

$$Y_k = \beta_0 + \beta_1(\text{Essential}_k) + \beta_2(\text{suburb}_k) + \beta_3(\text{town}_k) + \beta_4(\text{rural}_k) + \beta_5(\text{socioeconomic disadvantage}_k) + \beta_6(\text{socioeconomic advantage}_k) + \beta_7(\text{majority black}_k) + \beta_8(\text{majority Hispanic}_k) + \beta_9(\text{minority school}_k) + \beta_{10}(\text{mixed school}_k) + \beta_{11}(\text{size}_k) + \beta_{12}(\text{charter}_k) + \beta_{13}(\text{grade configuration}_k) + \beta_{14}(\text{initial value}_k) + \beta_{15}(\text{PPE}_k) + \beta_{16}(\text{district size}_k) + \beta_{17}(\text{number of schools in district}_k) + \beta_{18}(\text{district socioeconomic advantage}_k) + \beta_{19}(\text{district socioeconomic advantage}_k) + \beta_{20}(\text{district proportion black}_k) + \beta_{21}(\text{district proportion Hispanic}_k)$$

- Y_k is the outcome being analyzed. When we examine ISAT score gains, ISAT score levels, and time trends in attendance rates, the outcome is produced from the multilevel models discussed above.
- **Essential** represents one of the six essential support variables used in this analysis (effective leaders, collaborative teachers, involved families, supportive environment, and ambitious instruction, and an average of these essentials).
- **Suburb, town, and rural** are indicators for schools' urban location, with urban being the reference group. These are omitted for analyses of CPS schools.
- **Socioeconomic disadvantage** is the average of three statistics taken from the Common Core of Data (2010–11 and 2011–12 school years) and the 2007–11 American Community Survey (ACS): the percent of families below the poverty line in the school Census tract (converted into logits); the percent of males age 16 or higher who are jobless (converted into logits) in the school Census tract; and the percent of students in the school who are eligible for free or reduced-price lunch (also converted into logits). District socioeconomic disadvantage uses the same statistics but aggregated up at the district level.

---

50 While we used a multilevel model to estimate the time trend in attendance rates for each school, we opted to use OLS estimates instead of Empirical Bayes because the latter produced estimates that had extremely limited variability.

- **Socioeconomic advantage** is the average of two standardized statistics taken from the 2007–11 American Community Survey (ACS): the average years of education of adults 25 years or older in the school Census tract; and the percent of employed civilians in managerial and professional occupations (converted into logits). **District socioeconomic advantage** uses the same statistics but aggregated up at the district level.

- **Majority black, majority Hispanic, minority school, and mixed school** are indicators for school racial composition, based on the average of data from the Common Core of Data (CCD) for the school years of 2010–11 and 2011–12. To be majority black or majority Hispanic, a school had to have over half of their student body be African American or Hispanic. Minority schools are schools that are not majority black or majority Hispanic and have at least 33 percent of their student body black and Hispanic. Mixed schools are schools that are 67–89 percent Asian and white. The reference group is comprised of schools that are 90–100 percent Asian/white. For our analyses of CPS schools we only included the indicators for majority black and majority Hispanic, since most of the remaining schools were minority schools. At the district level, we used the same data to control for continuous measures of **district proportion black and district proportion Hispanic**.

- **Size** is the log enrollment of the school, based on the average of data from the Common Core of Data (CCD) for the school years of 2010–11 and 2011–12.

- **Charter** is an indicator for whether or not a school is a charter school.

- **Grade configuration** is an indicator for whether or not a school has enrolled students in the middle grades. Our analyses use elementary and high school outcomes, and schools serving students in the middle grades are represented in both kinds of outcomes. This variable is omitted in our analyses of K–5 schools.

- **Initial value** is included only for analyses examining change over time. When ISAT gains are examined, the initial value is the average of students' ISAT scores in 2011 (controlling for students' grade level), and when attendance change is examined, the initial value is the schools' attendance rate in 2011.

- **PPE** is the log of total per pupil expenditures of the school's district, averaged using data from the for the school years of 2010–11 and 2011–12. This is a district-level variable and is thus omitted for our analyses of CPS schools.

- **District size** is the log student enrollment in the school's district, averaged using data from the school year of 2010–11 and 2011–12.

- **Number of schools in district** is the log number of schools in the district, using data from the school year of 2011–12.

We evaluated these associations using standardized regression coefficients (also known as *"betas,"* presented in **Table A.6**). To isolate the association between the essential supports and student outcomes, we controlled for schools' socioeconomic context, their students' racial composition, urban location (CPS, non-CPS urban, suburban, rural, town), school size, charter status, and per pupil expenditures. Regression coefficients were standardized using standard deviations for *all* of Illinois.

As we explained in our report, we used the association between school socioeconomic disadvantage and student outcomes as a benchmark to evaluate the size of the relationship between the essential supports and outcomes. This benchmark association is statewide and thus calculated for all of Illinois (it was not calculated separately for CPS and non-CPS schools). The benchmark association is the standardized regression coefficient of socioeconomic disadvantage, controlling for school's urbanicity, log school size, charter status, and school grade configuration. For analyses where change over time is an outcome (learning gains and attendance rate trends), we also controlled for the school's 2011 value (i.e., 2011 average ISAT scores or attendance rates).

For attendance rate changes, socioeconomic disadvantage had nonsignificant effects for both elementary and high schools. When attendance change was an outcome, we chose 0.2 as a threshold for being a meaningful effect. This is based on Lipsey's (2012) review of effect sizes for education research; they conclude that 0.10 is the average effect size for schoolwide interventions (Lipsey, 2012, p. 36), and they point out that effect sizes for school-level analyses will be inflated by around 100 percent because of restricted variance in the outcome (Lipsey, 2012, p. 10).

Full Results

TABLE A.6

Fully Standardized Regression Coefficients ("betas") Showing Associations between Essential Supports and School Outcomes

		Average Essentials (beta)	Effective Leaders (beta)	Collaborative Teachers (beta)	Involved Families (beta)	Supportive Environment (beta)	Ambitious Instruction (beta)	Effect of Socioeconomic Disadvantage (beta)
ISAT Math Gains	Non-CPS	0.10*	0.02	0.05	0.09†	0.13*	0.10*	-0.17*
	CPS	0.12*	0.06†	0.10*	0.03	0.10*	0.14*	
	K-5	0.06†	0.05	0.04	0.09*			
ISAT Reading Gains	Non-CPS	0.15*	0.04	0.06†	0.20*	0.20*	0.20*	-0.14*
	CPS	0.07*	0.05	0.05†	0.02	0.04†	0.09*	
	K-5	0.04	0.03	0.02	0.07†			
ISAT Math Level	Non-CPS	0.12*	0.06*	0.11*	0.14*	0.06*	0.05*	-0.58*
	CPS	0.07*	0.00	0.07*	0.08†	0.06*	0.07*	
	K-5	0.12*	0.09†	0.11*	0.15*			
ISAT Reading Level	Non-CPS	0.11*	0.04*	0.09*	0.11*	0.07*	0.05*	-0.66*
	CPS	0.07*	0.00	0.07*	0.10*	0.05*	0.07*	
	K-5	0.12*	0.10*	0.12*	0.16*			
Attendance Rate Change (Elementary Schools)	Non-CPS	0.07*	0.05†	0.05†	0.08†	0.04	0.04	0.04†
	CPS	0.19*	0.11*	0.13*	0.18*	0.15*	0.18*	
	K-5	0.04	0.03	0.03	0.06*			
Attendance Rate Level (Elementary Schools)	Non-CPS	0.09*	0.03	0.08*	0.11*	0.05†	0.04	-0.43*
	CPS	0.03	-0.05	0.04	0.01	0.02	0.07*	
	K-5	0.07*	0.06*	.08*	0.09*			
Attendance Rate Change (High Schools)	Non-CPS	0.08*	0.03†	0.05*	0.09*	0.10*	0.08*	-0.03
	CPS	0.22*	0.16*	0.21*	0.30*	0.17*	0.15*	
Attendance Rate Level (High Schools)	Non-CPS	0.07*	0.01	0.06*	0.09*	0.11*	0.07*	-0.44*
	CPS	0.42*	0.20*	0.31*	0.43*	0.51*	0.45*	
Average ACT Score Level	Non-CPS	0.10*	0.02	0.07*	0.10*	0.18*	0.10*	-0.80*
	CPS	0.36*	0.16*	0.23*	0.32*	0.47*	0.41*	
Graduation Rate Level	Non-CPS	0.10*	0.03	0.06*	0.13*	0.16*	0.07*	-0.48*
	CPS	0.30*	0.14	0.22*	0.27*	0.36*	0.34*	

Note: * $p < .05$; † $p < .10$

TABLE A.7
Predicted Outcomes For Elementary Schools at 25th and 75th Percentiles of Essential Supports

	Average Essentials			Effective Leaders			Collaborative Teachers			Involved Families			Supportive Environment			Ambitious Instruction			Effect of Socioeconomic Disadvantage		
	Percentile		Difference	Percentile		Difference	Percentile		Difference	Percentile		Difference	Percentile		Difference	Percentile		Difference	Percentile		Difference
	25th	75th		25th	75th		25th	75th		25th	75th		25th	75th		25th	75th		25th	75th	
ISAT Math Gains																					
Non-CPS	10.3	10.8	0.5	10.4	10.5	0.1	10.3	10.6	0.3	10.3	10.8	0.5	10.0	10.6	0.6	10.1	10.6	0.5	11.3	10.5	-0.8
CPS	13.3	13.9	0.6	13.6	13.9	0.3	13.4	13.9	0.5	13.8	14.0	0.2	13.5	14.0	0.5	13.0	13.7	0.7			
K-5	11.8	12.1	0.3	11.9	12.2	0.3	11.9	12.1	0.2	11.6	12.1	0.5									
ISAT Reading Gains																					
Non-CPS	9.5	10.1	0.7	9.6	9.8	0.2	9.6	9.8	0.3	9.5	10.4	0.9	9.2	10.0	0.8	9.3	10.1	0.8	10.0	9.4	-0.6
CPS	12.1	12.4	0.3	12.2	12.4	0.2	12.2	12.4	0.2	12.4	12.4	0.1	12.2	12.4	0.2	12.0	12.3	0.4			
K-5	11.5	11.7	0.2	11.6	11.7	0.1	11.6	11.6	0.1	11.3	11.6	0.3									
ISAT Math Scores																					
Non-CPS	226.7	228.9	2.2	226.9	227.9	1.0	226.7	228.7	2.0	226.8	229.6	2.7	226.7	227.8	1.1	226.9	227.8	0.9	234.0	223.8	-10.2
CPS	235.5	236.8	1.3	236.8	236.8	0.0	235.5	236.8	1.3	236.0	237.4	1.5	235.8	236.9	1.1	235.2	236.4	1.2			
K-5	226.6	228.7	2.1	227.2	228.9	1.8	226.8	228.8	2.1	225.2	228.1	2.9									
ISAT Reading Scores																					
Non-CPS	216.8	218.5	1.7	216.9	217.6	0.7	216.8	218.2	1.4	216.9	218.7	1.8	216.8	217.9	1.0	217.1	217.8	0.7	223.1	213.2	-9.9
CPS	224.0	225.1	1.1	225.1	225.1	0.0	223.9	225.1	1.2	224.2	225.8	1.6	224.4	225.2	0.8	223.6	224.8	1.2			
K-5	217.4	219.3	1.9	217.9	219.5	1.6	217.6	219.4	1.8	216.1	218.8	2.7									
Attendance Rate Change, Elementary Schools																					
Non-CPS	0.04	0.08	0.05	0.04	0.07	0.03	0.04	0.07	0.03	0.04	0.10	0.06	0.05	0.07	0.03	0.05	0.08	0.03	0.02	0.05	0.03
CPS	-0.20	-0.07	0.13	-0.17	-0.09	0.08	-0.17	-0.08	0.08	-0.15	-0.02	0.13	-0.16	-0.06	0.10	-0.21	-0.10	0.12			
K-5	0.03	0.06	0.02	0.04	0.06	0.02	0.04	0.06	0.02	0.01	0.05	0.04									
Attendance Rate, Elementary Schools																					
Non-CPS	95.1	95.3	0.2	95.1	95.2	0.1	95.1	95.3	0.1	95.1	95.3	0.2	95.1	95.2	0.1	95.2	95.2	0.1	95.5	94.8	-0.7
CPS	95.2	95.3	0.1	95.4	95.3	-0.1	95.2	95.3	0.1	95.3	95.3	0.0	95.3	95.3	0.0	95.1	95.3	0.1			
K-5	95.2	95.3	0.1	95.2	95.4	0.1	95.2	95.4	0.1	95.1	95.5	0.2									

TABLE A.8

Predicted Outcomes For High Schools at 25th and 75th Percentiles of Essential Supports

	Average Essentials			Effective Leaders			Collaborative Teachers			Involved Families			Supportive Environment			Ambitious Instruction			Effect of Socioeconomic Disadvantage		
	Percentile		Difference	Percentile		Difference	Percentile		Difference	Percentile		Difference	Percentile		Difference	Percentile		Difference	Percentile		Difference
	25th	75th		25th	75th		25th	75th		25th	75th		25th	75th		25th	75th		25th	75th	
Attendance Rate Change																					
Non-CPS	-0.40	-0.25	0.15	-0.33	-0.28	0.05	-0.36	-0.27	0.09	-0.41	-0.24	0.17	-0.42	-0.24	0.18	-0.42	0.27	0.15	-0.18	-0.22	-0.04
CPS	-0.99	-0.59	0.40	-0.65	-0.36	0.30	-0.82	-0.43	0.39	-0.79	-0.23	0.56	-0.96	-0.65	0.31	-0.95	-0.69	0.27			
Attendance Rate Level																					
Non-CPS	91.8	92.3	0.5	92.0	92.1	0.1	91.9	92.3	0.4	91.8	92.4	0.6	91.7	92.4	0.7	91.8	92.2	0.4	93.4	91.3	-2.1
CPS	89.6	92.3	2.7	92.4	93.7	1.3	91.3	93.4	2.0	91.5	94.4	2.9	87.7	90.9	3.3	87.6	90.5	2.9			
Average ACT Score Level																					
Non-CPS	19.3	19.6	0.3	19.4	19.5	0.1	19.4	19.6	0.2	19.2	19.6	0.3	19.2	19.7	0.6	19.2	19.6	0.3	20.6	18.8	-1.8
CPS	18.5	19.6	1.1	19.7	20.2	0.5	19.4	20.1	0.7	19.4	20.5	1.1	17.5	19.0	1.5	17.6	18.8	1.3			
Four-Year Graduation Rate Level																					
Non-CPS	81.7	83.5	1.8	82.3	82.9	0.6	82.0	83.2	1.3	81.5	83.7	2.3	81.1	83.9	2.8	81.7	82.9	1.2	87.4	81.4	-6.0
CPS	75.2	80.4	5.2	80.8	83.2	2.4	78.7	82.5	3.8	79.6	84.2	4.6	71.7	77.9	6.2	71.2	76.9	5.7			

Appendix B

2013 5Essentials Survey Items By Essential and Individual Measure

1. EFFECTIVE LEADERS

A. Teacher Influence

Teacher Survey: How much influence do teachers have over school policy in each of the areas below:

1. Hiring new professional personnel.
2. Planning how discretionary school funds should be used.
3. Determining books and other instructional materials used in classrooms.
4. Setting standards for student behavior.
5. Establishing the curriculum and instructional program.
6. Determining the content of in-service programs.

Response Options: Not at All, A Little, Some, To a Great Extent

B. Principal Instructional Leadership

Teacher Survey: The principal at this school:

1. Participates in instructional planning with teams of teachers.
2. Knows what's going on in my classroom.
3. Carefully tracks student academic progress.
4. Understands how children learn.
5. Presses teachers to implement what they have learned in professional development.
6. Communicates a clear vision for our school.
7. Sets high standards for student learning.
8. Makes clear to the staff his or her expectations for meeting instructional goals.

Response Options: Strongly Disagree, Disagree, Agree, Strongly Agree

C. PGMC–Program Coherence

Teacher Survey: To what extent do you disagree or agree with the following:

1. Many special programs come and go at this school.
2. Once we start a new program, we follow up to make sure that it's working.
3. Curriculum, instruction, and learning materials are well coordinated across the different grade levels at this school.
4. We have so many different programs in this school that I can't keep track of them all.
5. There is consistency in curriculum, instruction, and learning materials among teachers in the same grade level at this school.

Response Options: Strongly Disagree, Disagree, Agree, Strongly Agree

D. Teacher-Principal Trust

Teacher Survey: Please mark the extent to which you disagree or agree with each of the following:

1. It's OK in this school to discuss feelings, worries, and frustrations with the principal.
2. The principal looks out for the personal welfare of the faculty members.
3. I trust the principal at his or her word.
4. The principal at this school is an effective manager who makes the school run smoothly.
5. The principal places the needs of children ahead of personal and political interests.
6. The principal has confidence in the expertise of the teachers.
7. The principal takes a personal interest in the professional development of teachers.
8. Teachers feel respected by the principal.

Response Options: Strongly Disagree, Disagree, Agree, Strongly Agree

2. COLLABORATIVE TEACHERS

A. Collective Responsibility

Teacher Survey: How many teachers in this school:

1. Feel responsible when students in this school fail.
2. Feel responsible to help each other do their best.
3. Help maintain discipline in the entire school, not just their classroom.
4. Take responsibility for improving the school.
5. Feel responsible for helping students develop self-control.
6. Feel responsible that all students learn.

Response Options: None, Some, About Half, Most, Nearly All

B. Quality Professional Development

Teacher Survey: Overall, my professional development experiences this year have:

1. Included opportunities to work productively with teachers from other schools.
2. Included enough time to think carefully about, try, and evaluate new ideas.
3. Been sustained and coherently focused, rather than short-term and unrelated.
4. Included opportunities to work productively with colleagues in my school.
5. Been closely connected to my school's improvement plan.

Response Options: Strongly Disagree, Disagree, Agree, Strongly Agree

C. School Commitment

Teacher Survey: Please mark the extent to which you disagree or agree with each of the following:

1. I wouldn't want to work in any other school.
2. I would recommend this school to parents seeking a place for their child.
3. I usually look forward to each working day at this school.
4. I feel loyal to this school.

Response Options: Strongly Disagree, Disagree, Agree, Strongly Agree

D. Teacher-Teacher Trust

Teacher Survey: Please mark the extent to which you disagree or agree with each of the following:

1. Teachers in this school trust each other.
2. It's OK in this school to discuss feelings, worries, and frustrations with other teachers.
3. Teachers respect other teachers who take the lead in school improvement efforts.
4. Teachers at this school respect those colleagues who are experts at their craft.
5. Teachers feel respected by other teachers.

Response Options: Strongly Disagree, Disagree, Agree, Strongly Agree

3. INVOLVED FAMILIES

A. Human & Social Resources in the Community

Student Survey: How much do you agree with the following statements about the community in which you live:

1. People in this neighborhood can be trusted.
2. The equipment and buildings in the neighborhood, park, or playground are well kept.
3. There are adults in this neighborhood that children can look up to.
4. Adults in this neighborhood know who the local children are.
5. During the day, it is safe for children to play in the local park or playground.

Response Options: Strongly Disagree, Disagree, Agree, Strongly Agree

B. Outreach to Parents

Teacher Survey: Please mark the extent to which you disagree or agree with each of the following:

1. Teachers work closely with parents to meet students' needs.
2. This school regularly communicates with parents about how they can help their children learn.
3. Teachers work at communicating to parents about support needed to advance the school mission.
4. Teachers encourage feedback from parents and the community.
5. The principal pushes teachers to communicate regularly with parents.
6. Teachers really try to understand parents' problems and concerns.
7. Parents are greeted warmly when they call or visit the school.

Response Options: Strongly Disagree, Disagree, Agree, Strongly Agree

C. Teacher-Parent Trust

Teacher Survey: Please mark the extent to which you disagree or agree with each of the following:

1. Parents do their best to help their children learn
2. Teachers feel good about parents' support for their work
3. Parents support teachers teaching efforts
4. Teachers and parents think of each other as partners in educating children.
5. Staff at this school work hard to build trusting relationships with parents.
6. Teachers feel respected by the parents of the students

Response Options: Strongly Disagree, Disagree, Agree, Strongly Agree

4. SUPPORTIVE ENVIRONMENT

A. Peer Support for Academic Work

Student Survey: How many of the students in your [target] class:

1. Think doing homework is important.
2. Feel it is important to pay attention in class.
3. Feel it is important to come to school every day.
4. Try hard to get good grades.

Response Options: None, A Few, About Half, Most, Nearly All

B. Academic Personalism

**Student Survey: How much do you agree with the following statements about your [TARGET] class:
The teacher for this class:**

1. Helps me catch up if I am behind.
2. Notices if I have trouble learning something.
3. Gives me specific suggestions about how I can improve my work in this class.
4. Is willing to give extra help on schoolwork if I need it.
5. Explains things in a different way if I don't understand something in class.

Response Options: Strongly Disagree, Disagree, Agree, Strongly Agree

C. Academic Press

Student Survey: In my [target] class, how often:

1. The teacher asks difficult questions in class.
2. The teacher asks difficult questions on tests.
3. This class challenges me.
4. This class requires me to work hard to do well.

   Response Options: Never, Once In a While, Most of the Time, All the Time

How much do you agree with the following statements about your [target] class:

5. This class really makes me think.
6. I really learn a lot in this class.

   Response Options: Strongly Disagree, Disagree, Agree, Strongly Agree

In my [target] class, my teacher:

7. The teacher wants us to become better thinkers, not just memorize things.
8. The teacher expects me to do my best all the time.
9. The teacher expects everyone to work hard.

   Response Options: Strongly Disagree, Disagree, Agree, Strongly Agree

D. Safety

Student Survey: How safe do you feel:

1. Outside around the school.
2. Traveling between home and school.
3. In the hallways and bathrooms of the school.
4. In their classes

   Response Options: Not Safe, Somewhat Safe, Mostly Safe, Very Safe

E. Student-Teacher Trust

Student Survey: How much do you agree with the following:

1. My teachers always keep their promises
2. I feel safe and comfortable with my teachers at this school.
3. My teachers will always listen to students' ideas.
4. When my teachers tell me not to do something, I know they have a good reason
5. My teachers treat me with respect.

   Response Options: Strongly Disagree, Disagree, Agree, Strongly Agree

F. School-Wide Future Orientation (H.S. Only)

Student Survey: How much do you agree with the following. At my high school:

1. Teachers work hard to make sure that students stay in school.
2. Teachers pay attention to all students, not just the top students.
3. Teachers make sure that all students are planning for life after graduation.
4. Teachers work hard to make sure that all students are learning.
5. All students are encouraged to go to college.
6. High school is seen as preparation for the future.

   Response Options: Strongly Disagree, Disagree, Agree, Strongly Agree

G. Expectations for Postsecondary Education (H.S. Only):

Teacher Survey: Please mark the extent to which you disagree or agree with each of the following:

1. Most of the students in this school are planning to go to college.
2. Teachers expect most students in this school to go to college.
3. Teachers at this school help students plan for college outside of class time.
4. The curriculum at this school is focused on helping students get ready for college.
5. Teachers in this school feel that it is a part of their job to prepare students to succeed in college.

   Response Options: Strongly Disagree, Disagree, Agree, Strongly Agree

5. AMBITIOUS INSTRUCTION

A. Course Clarity

Student Survey: How much do you agree with the following statements about your [target] class:

1. I learn a lot from feedback on my work.
2. The homework assignments help me to learn the course material.
3. The work we do in class is good preparation for the test.
4. I know what my teacher wants me to learn in this class.
5. It's clear to me what I need to do to get a good grade.

Response Options: Strongly Disagree, Disagree, Agree, Strongly Agree

B. English Instruction

Students Survey: In your ENGLISH/READING/LITERATURE class this year, how often do you do the following:

1. Rewrite a paper or essay in response to comments.
2. Improve a piece of writing as a class or with partners.
3. Debate the meaning of a reading.
4. Discuss how culture, time, or place affects an author's writing.
5. Discuss connections between a reading and real life people

Response Options: Never, Once or Twice a Semester, Once or Twice a Month, Once or Twice a Week, Almost Every Day

C. Math Instruction

Student Survey: In your MATH class this year, how often do you do the following:

1. Write a math problem for other students to solve.
2. Write a few sentences to explain how you solved a math problem.
3. Apply math to situations in life outside of school.
4. Explain how you solved a problem to the class.
5. Discuss possible solutions to problems with other students.

Response Options: Never, Once or Twice a Semester, Once or Twice a Month, Once or Twice a Week, Almost Every Day

D. Quality of Student Discussion

Teacher Survey: To what extent do the following characteristics describe discussions that occur in your class:

1. Students use data and text references to support their ideas.
2. Students provide constructive feedback to their peers/teachers.
3. Students build on each other's ideas during discussion.
4. Most students participate in the discussion at some point.
5. Students show each other respect.

Response Options: Never, Rarely, Sometimes, Almost Always

ABOUT THE AUTHORS

JOSHUA KLUGMAN is a Senior Quantitative Research Analyst at UChicago CCSR. His current research focuses on the effects of the essential supports on student outcomes and the role of noncognitive factors in students' academic performance. Previously he was Assistant Professor of Sociology at Temple University. He earned a BA in Sociology at Northwestern University and a PhD in Sociology at Indiana University.

MOLLY F. GORDON is a Senior Research Analyst at UChicago CCSR. Her current research focuses on the impact of closing schools on families, examining the 5Essential supports surveys across Illinois, and investigating how school leadership influences instruction and student learning. Previously, she was a Research Associate at the Center for Applied Research and Educational Improvement (CAREI) at the University of Minnesota. She earned a BA in Philosophy and an MA in Educational Policy Studies from the University of Wisconsin–Madison, and a PhD in Educational Policy and Administration from the University of Minnesota–Twin Cities.

PENNY BENDER SEBRING is a Senior Research Associate at the University of Chicago and Co-Founder of the Consortium on Chicago School Research, at the University's Urban Education Institute. She is an author of *Teens, Digital Media, and the Chicago Public Library* and the book *Organizing Schools for Improvement: Lessons from Chicago*. Dr. Sebring graduated from Grinnell College, following which she was a Peace Corps volunteer and high school teacher. She received her PhD in Education and Social Policy from Northwestern University. She is currently a Life Trustee of Grinnell; chair of the Policy Advisory Board for Northwestern's School of Education and Social Policy; and a member of the board of directors for the Chicago Public Education Fund. Dr. Sebring has received an Alumni Merit Award from Northwestern; the John J. Dugan Award from OneGoal; the Stanley C. Golder Community Service Award from the Golden Apple Foundation; and a Community Service award from the Associated Colleges of Illinois.

SUSAN E. SPORTE is the Director of Research Operations at the University of Chicago Consortium on Chicago School Research. Her research focuses on teacher effectiveness, teacher preparation, and the organization of schools. Sporte holds a BS from Michigan State University, an MA from the University of Illinois at Springfield, and an MA and EdD from the Harvard Graduate School of Education.

This report reflects the interpretation of the authors. Although UChicago CCSR's Steering Committee provided technical advice, no formal endorsement by these individuals, organizations, or the full Consortium should be assumed.

UCHICAGO CCSR

CONSORTIUM ON CHICAGO SCHOOL RESEARCH

Directors

ELAINE M. ALLENSWORTH
Lewis-Sebring Director

EMILY KRONE
Director for Outreach and Communication

JENNY NAGAOKA
Deputy Director

MELISSA RODERICK
Senior Director
Hermon Dunlap Smith Professor
School of Social Service Administration

PENNY BENDER SEBRING
Co-Founder

SUSAN E. SPORTE
Director for Research Operations

MARISA DE LA TORRE
Director for Internal Research Capacity

Steering Committee

KATHLEEN ST. LOUIS CALIENTO
Co-Chair
Spark, Chicago

KIM ZALENT
Co-Chair
Business and Professional People for the Public Interest

Ex-Officio Members

SARA RAY STOELINGA
Urban Education Institute

Institutional Members

JOHN R. BARKER
Chicago Public Schools

CLARICE BERRY
Chicago Principals and Administrators Association

AARTI DHUPELIA
Chicago Public Schools

KAREN G.J. LEWIS
Chicago Teachers Union

SHERRY J. ULERY
Chicago Public Schools

Individual Members

VERONICA ANDERSON
Communications Consultant

JOANNA BROWN
Logan Square Neighborhood Association

CATHERINE DEUTSCH
Illinois Network of Charter Schools

RAQUEL FARMER-HINTON
University of Wisconsin, Milwaukee

KIRABO JACKSON
Northwestern University

CHRIS JONES
Stephen T. Mather High School

DENNIS LACEWELL
Urban Prep Charter Academy for Young Men

LILA LEFF
Umoja Student Development Corporation

RUANDA GARTH MCCULLOUGH
Young Women's Leadership Academy

LUISIANA MELÉNDEZ
Erikson Institute

CRISTINA PACIONE-ZAYAS
Latino Policy Forum

PAIGE PONDER
One Million Degrees

LUIS R. SORIA
Chicago Public Schools

BRIAN SPITTLE
DePaul University

MATTHEW STAGNER
Mathematica Policy Research

AMY TREADWELL
Chicago New Teacher Center

ERIN UNANDER
Al Raby High School

ARIE J. VAN DER PLOEG
American Institutes for Research (Retired)

www.ingramcontent.com/pod-product-compliance
Lightning Source LLC
Chambersburg PA
CBHW060821090426

42738CB00002B/66